MW00582543

by Tony Glazer

A SAMUEL FRENCH ACTING EDITION

SAMUEL
FRENCH
FOUNDED 1830

NEW YORK HOLLYWOOD LONDON TORONTO

SAMUELFRENCH.COM

IMPORTANT BILLING AND CREDIT
REQUIREMENTS

All producers of *STAIN must* give credit to the Author of the Play in all programs distributed in connection with performances of the Play, and in all instances in which the title of the Play appears for the purposes of advertising, publicizing or otherwise exploiting the Play and/or a production. The name of the Author *must* appear on a separate line on which no other name appears, immediately following the title and *must* appear in size of type not less than fifty percent of the size of the title type.

STAIN was first produced Off-Broadway by Choice Theatricals on July 23rd, 2008 at the Kirk Theatre on Theatre Row. The play was directed by Scott C. Embler, with Jennifer Ganske as assistant director, and Cheryl Dennis as the general manager. Scenic design was by Eddy Trotter, costume design was by Cully Long, lighting design was by Nick Kolin, fight choreography was by B.H. Barry, sound design and original musical score were by Andrew Eisele. Press was handled by Joe Trentacosta, Springer Associates. Abby Marcus handled PR and marketing. The production stage manager was Barbara Janice Kielhofer, with Andrea Jess Berkey as assistant stage manager. The show was performed with the following cast:

THOMAS . . . . Tobias Segal

ARTHUR . . . . .Jim O'Connor

JULIA. . . . . .Summer Crockett Moore

THERESA. . . . . .Joanna Bayless

CARLA. . . . . Karina Arroyave

GEORGE . . . . .Peter Brensinger

CHARACTERS

THOMAS - 15 years old.

ARTHUR - 40s, Father of Thomas.

JULIA - 30s, Mother of Thomas.

THERESA - 50s Mother of Julia.

GEORGE - 15 years old, friend of Thomas.

CARLA - 32 years old, lawyer of Puerto Rican descent.

AUTHOR'S NOTE

STAIN was originally performed with one ten-minute intermission. However, it is possible, and permissible, for future productions to perform this piece without an intermission.

   - T.G.

ACT ONE

Scene One

*(Lights up on **ARTHUR** and **THOMAS**, Arthur's son, as they sit on a park bench – sleazy, bad neighborhood. Grey day. They eat hot dogs, Arthur's drowning in relish and sauerkraut. Thomas's hot dog is plain – no ketchup, mustard, nothing.)*

ARTHUR. I don't know how you eat that plain, Thomas.

THOMAS. Tastes good.

ARTHUR. Rat hair gets in these, you know?

THOMAS. You told me.

ARTHUR. What?

THOMAS. You told me that last Sunday.

ARTHUR. They don't call it rat hair on the package of ingredients. They called it "ash" in my day. Not sure what they call it now. They may not have to mention it anymore, the rat hair. But it's in there, don't kid yourself.

THOMAS. I know, you said.

*(**ARTHUR** doesn't respond. They resume eating in silence. In the distance a gunshot rings out. They have no reaction – they've heard things like this before.)*

ARTHUR. So. You have a new girlfriend these days?

THOMAS. Yes.

ARTHUR. She white?

THOMAS. Yes.

ARTHUR. I'm proud of you.

THOMAS. Thanks, Dad.

*(**ARTHUR** looks over to **THOMAS**, a bit apprehensive, then...)*

ARTHUR. You're over the whole "black" thing, then?

THOMAS. Puerto Rican.

7

ARTHUR. What's that?

THOMAS. She was Puerto Rican. She wasn't black.

ARTHUR. Dark skin, "person of color" – your "minority phase" – you over that?

THOMAS. *(shrugging)* I guess.

ARTHUR. Good. That's good.

(Again they eat their hot dogs in quiet. Until...)

I'm not racist, you know?

THOMAS. Uh-huh.

ARTHUR. This is the park of my youth. I used to come here when I was a little boy. When I was your age it was just people like us. Now...everyone's here...and not all for the better but I still come regardless of how "colored up" it is.

THOMAS. Sure.

*(**ARTHUR** looks over to **THOMAS**.)*

ARTHUR. It's just all that interracial stuff, T...it's a lot of trouble you don't need. People see you together on the street, these streets...this park, even...

(beat)

Besides, financially speaking, you don't want some welfare "Latina" hooking her kids onto your wagon and –

THOMAS. She's a lawyer.

ARTHUR. What?

THOMAS. She doesn't have any kids and she's a lawyer. She makes more money than you, actually.

ARTHUR. I make good money in retail.

THOMAS. "Lawyer" good?

*(Silence. They go back to their hotdogs. **ARTHUR** stews until...)*

ARTHUR. Well, we ended that nonsense with her, so that's good.

THOMAS. She didn't want to see me anymore, either.

ARTHUR. Fucking nerve, fucking queen bee. Why wouldn't she want to see you?

THOMAS. I'm only fifteen.

ARTHUR. Spanish whore.

THOMAS. Legally it was a problem for her.

ARTHUR. Pedophile. You should turn her in to the police... dirty, black, pedophile bitch. Who the cunt does she think she is?

THOMAS. I'd rather just let it go, Dad. I'm the one who lied to her. I told her I was much older.

ARTHUR. Don't do that, T. Don't ever put yourself down like that. You got nothing to be sorry about. You don't need to apologize to her, to me... *anyone*. Never say you're sorry.

THOMAS. Okay.

ARTHUR. You start apologizing, it never ends. People expect it. You say you're sorry and then everyone shits on you. Promise me you won't do that. Ever.

THOMAS. I promise.

ARTHUR. Good.

(More quiet. More hot dogs.)

(Finally...)

ARTHUR. *(cont.)* This new girl. You like her?

THOMAS. She's okay.

ARTHUR. How much do you like her?

THOMAS. *(shrugging)* I don't know. It's too soon. She's okay.

ARTHUR. All women fall into three different categories, just between you and me.

THOMAS. They do?

ARTHUR. *(nodding)* You got your "ecto-plasm girls" – they're just holes you cum in. You go to them mostly 'cause they're there and it's easy; less to think about, convenient. You got your "fuck buddies" – they're your friends and you cum in them, too, but you don't mind them hanging around either. It's just sex, though, that's all it will ever be – for them, too. Then there's the "special ones" – you marry those.

THOMAS. Was Mom special? You married her.

ARTHUR. I did. She was.

THOMAS. Did she stop being special?

(No answer.)

ARTHUR. This new girl. If you had to guess…

THOMAS. I really don't know, Dad.

ARTHUR. Okay, okay. You're right. Too soon to tell. You shouldn't rush it anyway. All things at their own pace.

(Pause. More hot dogs and then…)

"Ectoplasm girls" are fine but you have to be careful.

THOMAS. How come?

ARTHUR. It's so easy with them, you can end up with a lot of them. You can get used to being with them, 'cause they're always around. But if you fuck too many of those they'll leave a mark on you – they'll leave a stain.

THOMAS. A stain?

ARTHUR. That stain won't come off, either. It's like a tattoo…a tattoo stain you'll always have to deal with and if you fuck too many of them after that, you'll have stains all over. You'll never find a good girl at that point, you'll never find the "special one" – the ones you marry – because they'll see your stain coming a mile away. Even your "fuck buddies," the sport fuckers will stay away.

THOMAS. Oh.

ARTHUR. You being careful? With the sex? I mean, you don't have any diseases now, do you?

THOMAS. I don't think so.

ARTHUR. You use a rubber, right?

THOMAS. Sometimes.

ARTHUR. You used one with the "darkie?"

THOMAS. She had a cervical cap.

ARTHUR. What's that?

THOMAS. It's like a rubber stopper.

ARTHUR. A what?

THOMAS. A stopper, a plug. It's like a little rubber plug that covers the cervix so she doesn't get pregnant.

ARTHUR. Does that stop diseases?

THOMAS. No.

ARTHUR. Cat shit, Thomas. You have to go get a test, now. You don't know where that woman –

THOMAS. I'm fine.

ARTHUR. Fine, nothing. You could have…AIDS inside you or…

THOMAS. I miss it.

ARTHUR. *(not listening)* …or worse. I mean –

THOMAS. I miss her cervical cap, sometimes.

ARTHUR. What?

THOMAS. Sometimes I miss it.

ARTHUR. Miss what?

THOMAS. Her cervical cap.

ARTHUR. Thomas, I'm trying to tell you something important here.

THOMAS. I'd be going down on her, really getting in there and I'd…feel it.

ARTHUR. Jesus.

THOMAS. It would be so strange, too, in the middle of all that hot, heavy sweatiness to taste this tiny, rubber stopper.

ARTHUR. I don't need to…*Jesus*, Thomas. I mean…*Jesus*.

THOMAS. But now…I miss it.

(beat)

ARTHUR. It'll pass.

THOMAS. You think?

ARTHUR. I do. Things pass.

THOMAS. Like Mom?

(**ARTHUR** *does not respond.*)

Why did you two get divorced?

ARTHUR. What did your Mom say?

THOMAS. She didn't. She won't.

ARTHUR. Oh.

(Another gunshot – this one farther away. Again neither has any response.)

Don't go down on them too much.

THOMAS. I like it.

ARTHUR. That's fine to like it, it's healthy. I'm not so sure it's age appropriate at the moment but it's normal to like it. Just don't do it too much. You do it too much they'll start expecting it all the time and you miss it once it's gonna be, "Why don't you go down on me anymore? Why don't we ever go dancing? Shoes go in the shoe tree!"

(beat)

It's not worth it, trust me.

THOMAS. Okay.

ARTHUR. And promise me you'll get an AIDS test this week.

THOMAS. I promise.

ARTHUR. Go to the free clinic, the anonymous ones downtown. Don't check with the family doctor they'll think you're "homo-we gay-go." Can barely pay your insurance premiums as it is. Those queers have the highest premiums in the world. Worse than the chinks – the *chinks,* Christ.

(ARTHUR goes to eat the rest of his hot dog but has suddenly lost appetite. He throws the unfinished hot dog in the trash can.)

Puerto Rican cervical cap, huh?

THOMAS. I think about it sometimes.

ARTHUR. Well, don't. Don't give it any energy. You don't give it any energy, it doesn't exist. You got that?

(THOMAS attempts to think it through.)

THOMAS. *(not understanding)* Well…I mean…are you saying…

(**ARTHUR** *checks the time on his watch.*)

ARTHUR. Just finish your hot dog, T.

THOMAS. Okay.

(**ARTHUR** *checks his watch, realizing the time.*)

ARTHUR. *(looking at his watch)* Gotta get you back before your Mother has an ulcer all over me.

(Lights out.)

Scene Two

(One hour later.)

(Lights up on the dining room/living room area of a very well put together home – not luxuriant but not middle class either. **JULIA** *and her mother,* **THERESA,** *are setting the dining table for dinner. They are setting three places.* **THERESA** *notices how tense* **JULIA** *is becoming.)*

JULIA. He keeps him late just to get back at me. It's like he's always trying to have the last word without ever opening his mouth. Crazy. He just makes me crazy, sometimes.

THERESA. Try not to let it bother you, dear. I don't.

JULIA. Well, why would you, Mother? I mean, honestly. You didn't marry him. You didn't sit through a nasty divorce. You're not currently raising a child with him. Why would you let it bother you?

THERESA. *(nonplussed)* Try not to let me bother you, dear. I don't.

*(***JULIA** *stops setting the table for a moment and looks at her mother – something's not right.* **THERESA** *sensing that her daughter is looking at her, smiles.)*

JULIA. What have you done?

THERESA. I haven't the slightest idea what you're talking about.

JULIA. You know exactly what I'm talking about. Did you have it done?

THERESA. Julia, a lady never discusses these things. I brought you up better than that. I'm sure of it.

JULIA. We had a long conversation about how you shouldn't be doing things like this.

THERESA. Oh, for heaven's sake, Julia, it's not a sin. I'm not filleting children. I had a little Botox.

JULIA. No Botox. We agreed. You have more important health issues to consider than that. You have high blood pressure.

THERESA. I have crows feet. Well, I *had* anyway. I think Dr. Thompson's work speaks for itself.

(Despite herself, **JULIA** *is impressed.)*

JULIA. *(jealous)* It does look good.

THERESA. This is my point, Julia. Time or Tuck. Nature or needle. These are the choices for the modern, enlightened woman and the cruel indignities her face must face.

JULIA. It's called aging.

THERESA. Well, I don't like it. I'm not a wine or a cheese. I'm a perfectly fine specimen of a woman who still has a few more years of random dating left in her before the doors shut completely.

JULIA. I really can't hear this.

THERESA. You should be out there, too. It's been three years since you two split. Divorce doesn't mean dead. Just because you and Arthur are no longer together, it doesn't mean you have to shut off your need for sexual contact. We are all sexual beings.

JULIA. *(skeptical)* Please.

THERESA. It's true.

JULIA. When have you been a sexual being since Dad died?

THERESA. This morning. Seven-forty five with the massage option on the shower head.

JULIA. Dear God.

THERESA. I'm still working my way up to an actual person. For now, water sex will have to suffice.

JULIA. You're making me ill.

THERESA. He got the house when you left, Julia. Not your clitoris.

JULIA. Mother!

THERESA. Well, I'm sorry. But as long as this machine of mine still has the ability to self-lubricate without an army of petroleum products I am going to take full advantage of it. And you should, too.

JULIA. I can't believe you still go to church with that mouth.

THERESA. Every Sunday. Front row, center.

JULIA. You've crossed a line.

THERESA. Really? Which part? Celebrating my body's ability to "self-lubricate" or the word "clitoris?"

JULIA. Would you stop?

THERESA. No, I won't. "Self-lubricate, self-lubricate!"

JULIA. This is abuse.

THERESA. "Clitoris, clitoris, clitoris!"

*(**THOMAS** enters hearing only part of the conversation.)*

THOMAS. Who's "hit or miss?"

THERESA. *(without missing a beat)* Well, if you must know –

JULIA. No one. Thank you very much.

*(**JULIA** shoots her mother the "evil eye" and **THERESA** relents.)*

THERESA. How are you, dear?

THOMAS. I'm fine. Sorry I'm late.

*(**THERESA** gives him a big hug and a kiss.)*

JULIA. Do you know what time it is?

THOMAS. He wouldn't stop talking.

*(**THOMAS** immediately begins helping his mother set the table. She gives him a kiss on the forehead despite her annoyance.)*

THERESA. Men will do that. I'm so sorry to break this to you Thomas, but you originate from a chromosome just toxic with "talkers." It is one of the many crosses your sex will have to bear.

*(**THOMAS** hardly registers **THERESA**'s comments – he's heard them all before.)*

THOMAS. That's okay, Grandma. I like talking.

*(**THOMAS** gives **THERESA** a peck on the cheek.)*

THERESA. What did I tell you about that, young man?

THOMAS. Sorry…Theresa.

THERESA. Thank you, dear.

THOMAS. You're welcome. Looking good around the eyes.

(JULIA *looks on, annoyed* THOMAS *was privy to this information.*)

THERESA. Sweet boy. You noticed.

(THERESA *and* THOMAS *share a smile.* THOMAS *continues to help his mother set the table.*)

JULIA. What was he talking about that was so important he had to make you late?

THOMAS. Women.

THERESA. He is the expert.

JULIA. What did he say?

THOMAS. He said there are three different kinds.

JULIA. Of women? Only three?

THOMAS. That's what he said.

JULIA. *(preparing for the worst)* Okay. Let's hear it.

THOMAS. *(hesitant)* It's a little rude.

THERESA. Can't be that bad.

THOMAS. There's the "ecto-plasm girls," "fuck buddies" and "special ones."

THERESA. Ah-ha.

JULIA. Go on.

THOMAS. *(remembering)* The "ecto-plasm girls" are just the ones you…deposit stuff into, the "fuck buddies", also known as "sport fuckers," are the ones you also…make deposits in…but you also have fun with them even though you're just friends and the "special ones" are the ones you marry.

(*They all sit around the table and begin dinner.*)

THERESA. Care to take a guess which category you were in, Julia?

THOMAS. Oh, he said you were a "special one."

THERESA. Imagine that.

THOMAS. But you're not married anymore.

THERESA. Nothing gets by you, Thomas.

THOMAS. I asked him if you stopped being a "special one" because you're not married anymore. I asked him what changed it.

(*awkward silence*)

JULIA. (*tense*) What did he say?

THOMAS. He didn't. He wouldn't tell me anything.

(*more awkward silence*)

Does anyone here have anything to add?

(*Nothing.* **THERESA** *and* **JULIA** *share a weighted look.* **THOMAS** *sees this and is not happy about it.*)

Nothing? Okay. I'd like to go on the record as saying how frustrating it is that on a "day to day" basis I am inundated with non-requested information by all the supervising adults in my life but when it comes to things I'd like you to speak with me about, all I get is silence.

THERESA. Noted. It will be entered into the family minutes under the heading, "Things that will ultimately scar Thomas for life."

THOMAS. Why can't I know?

JULIA. Some things just happen.

THOMAS. Oh, gee, that sounds interesting. Tell me about it.

JULIA. When you're older.

THOMAS. Anytime you don't want to talk to me about something you always say "when you're older" but "older" never comes.

THERESA. It'll creep up on you, dear.

THOMAS. I want to know.

JULIA. When you're older –

THOMAS. Stop it. When I'm older I'll just be angry that you didn't tell me sooner.

THERESA. Don't interrupt your mother, Thomas. No one likes rudeness.

THOMAS. No one likes being kept out of the loop either but all three of you seem to think that's a good idea.

JULIA. Your father didn't leave because of you or anything that you did. You shouldn't blame yourself.

THOMAS. I don't.

THERESA. Of course you do, darling. All children blame themselves when their parents split.

THOMAS. But I don't.

THERESA. Well, maybe you should.

JULIA. Mother!

THERESA. Seriously, try giving it shot.

THOMAS. You want me to blame myself, so that you can tell me not to blame myself?

THERESA. It would give us more to do as a family.

THOMAS. Meals and weekends aren't enough?

THERESA. Nothing is ever enough. My appetite for family time is insatiable.

(**THERESA** *jokingly makes "eating sounds" as though she were a hungry zombie.*)

JULIA. *(to* **THERESA***)* Stop helping me, please.

THOMAS. I want to know why.

JULIA. What's this sudden desire to know?

THOMAS. It's been three years. I think I should know.

JULIA. *(paranoid)* Did your father say something? Did he insinuate something?

THOMAS. No, I already told you, no one tells me a thing. That's the problem. Why can't you just talk to me about this?

JULIA. No.

THOMAS. But –

JULIA. The answer's no, Thomas.

THOMAS. Mom.

JULIA. *(erupting)* Not tonight. I don't want to talk about this right now. *Enough.*

(Tension hangs there a moment until…)

THOMAS. When you two divorced and we came here, you told me that I was going to have to act more like an adult than a teenager and I accepted my end of the deal. But not telling me the truth makes what you say dishonest. You can't have it both ways. You want me to be an adult? Start treating me like one.

(Silence. It's clear to THOMAS *that no one is going to address this topic.)*

Fine.

(They all sit down and begin eating. Until…)

Pass the vegetables, please, Grandma.

*(*THERESA, *acknowledging* THOMAS' *dig, passes a bowl of vegetables to* THOMAS *and he spoons some food onto his plate. The family begins to eat in silence.)*

(Lights out.)

Scene Three

*(Lights up on **THOMAS** and his friend, **GEORGE**. It is a couple of days later. They seem to be in another part of the same park. This part of the park seems even dirtier, if that's possible. Crack vials and chicken bones litter the ground.)*

THOMAS. Why would you want to take steroids?

GEORGE. *(matter of fact)* Get huge. Break stuff.

THOMAS. *(motioning to **GEORGE**'s crotch)* I heard it makes you tiny in other places which might be a real problem for you 'cause you're already in a deficit down there.

GEORGE. Peeking at me when I get dressed?

THOMAS. Your mom told me.

GEORGE. Hairless ferret.

THOMAS. Pinky knob.

*(After a beat he and **THOMAS** begin to playfully punch each other back and forth.)*

GEORGE. Scat muncher.

THOMAS. Ass knocker.

GEORGE. Fart sniffer.

THOMAS. Gas master.

GEORGE. Ball licker.

THOMAS. Cum guzzling blood knot.

GEORGE. *(immediately grossed out)* Okay, okay, stop, that's, that's just…*gross*, Thomas.

(They laugh, rub their shoulders which are now smarting.)

THOMAS. Seriously, steroids are kind of unhealthy.

GEORGE. I just want to get huge and rage. What's the big deal? Doesn't anyone rage anymore? Country's all backwards.

THOMAS. Your mom's backwards.

(Another beat. And then the two begin playfully punching each other again.)

GEORGE. Dick whistle.

THOMAS. Pussy face.

GEORGE. Elephant nut.

THOMAS. Blood fart.

GEORGE. Monkey tit.

THOMAS. Smeg felcher.

GEORGE. Snot sipper.

THOMAS. Vaginal yeast soup enema.

GEORGE. *(even more grossed out than before) Mother of…*what the hell kind of web sites are you surfing?

THOMAS. Yoursister.com.

GEORGE. Spending too much time with your Dad is the problem.

(They rub their shoulders which are now very sore. **GEORGE** *pulls out a joint from behind his ear and begins digging in his pocket for matches.)*

THOMAS. He's not so bad. I only see him on Sundays. He takes me to R rated movies, buys me hot dogs, I listen to him talk, then I go home. There's really not much to it.

GEORGE. Yeah, but he's like a demon.

THOMAS. He's not like a demon.

*(***GEORGE*** lights up the joint and begins puffing hard on it. He sucks in a nice long champion's drag and passes it to* **THOMAS** *who takes and inhales a hit of his own and passes it back to* **GEORGE** *who takes another hit.)*

THOMAS. *(cont.) Demons* are like…demons. He's just a…

GEORGE. *(exhaling)* Dick.

THOMAS. I guess.

GEORGE. Didn't he hit her?

THOMAS. Once. Right before we moved out. He started drinking a lot and just wound up and gave her the pimp hand.

GEORGE. Case in point.

THOMAS. He said he felt bad about it.

GEORGE. So he says.

THOMAS. Of course, he didn't feel bad enough to move out himself. I had to leave my bedroom which was so much better than the one I'm in now. And, to make things worse, every once in a while he'll talk about it. Like, "Your bedroom's still there, Thomas. Exactly how you left it. Just so you know."

GEORGE. You still don't know why they split?

THOMAS. Neither of them will tell me.

GEORGE. Your grandmother's cool, though, yeah?

THOMAS. Yeah, she's pretty cool. I never knew my grandfather, but she's a lot cooler than both my mom and dad.

GEORGE. At least you got that.

THOMAS. But even she won't tell me about their divorce. Maybe she doesn't know. I mean, I didn't even know who she was until after the divorce and we moved in. But she must know something and she won't say a thing. No one wants to talk about it – it's such amazing crap. My dad's the worst about it, too. At least my mom will try to offer up some kind of reason about why I can't know. My dad just shuts down. Useless.

GEORGE. Why do you even bother meeting him on Sundays? You should refuse until they tell you. You know, go on strike.

THOMAS. I can't. I think a judge made the order. Wrote it down somewhere.

GEORGE. You can't say "no?"

THOMAS. I guess I could but I feel like I'm supposed to do this for him. Like it makes him feel better about things. The divorce. Us moving out.

GEORGE. Yeah, but how does being there make you feel?

THOMAS. Who are you, my therapist now?

GEORGE. *(passing the joint)* Yes, call me Dr. George. Here's your medication, Thomas. Toke this and all will be pleasantly viewed through the rose tinted world of THC.

THOMAS. Does my insurance cover this?

GEORGE. There may be a "prison related co-pay somewhere along the bottom line."

THOMAS. Always read the fine print.

GEORGE. Yup.

(They smoke some more in silence. A gunshot rings out. **THOMAS** *and* **GEORGE** *do not respond to it.)*

He was such a racist about Carla, too.

THOMAS. He was just being protective. The whole "age thing."

GEORGE. Everything out of his mouth was "black bitch" this and "spic whore" that. He almost hemorrhaged when he heard about her.

THOMAS. It wasn't that bad.

GEORGE. Then why do you have to make up some story about having a "new white girlfriend" just to get him to leave you alone about it?

*(***THOMAS** *doesn't answer. They smoke some more. Finally...)*

How long has it been since you've seen her?

THOMAS. Couple months.

GEORGE. She was hot.

THOMAS. I know. I was there, George. And you shouldn't have been spying on me just because you forgot to bring your fake ID.

GEORGE. I know, I know but I was just in awe the night you met her, bro. How you walked right up to her at that bar, started talking to her.

THOMAS. That was pretty ballsy, huh?

GEORGE. That's what I'm saying, guitar hero.

(They smoke.)

THOMAS. I left a bunch of voice-mail messages on her cell phone, apologizing for lying...getting my mom involved.... but it got weird once she knew...

GEORGE. Yeah…but the sex. Off the grid, right?

THOMAS. *(mocking)* Yes, George. It was very "off the grid."

GEORGE. *(laughing)* Bastard.

THOMAS. *(laughing)* That's me.

> *(Their laughter dies down until the two just stare out, stoned.)*
>
> *(Finally…***THOMAS** *checks his watch.)*

THOMAS. *(cont.)* We should get back.

GEORGE. No one's missing us right now.

THOMAS. Not true. I think we're both very miss-able.

GEORGE. I can't navigate Chemistry class with chemicals in me.

THOMAS. Stop whining. By the time we get back, it'll be gym.

GEORGE. I can't climb a rope in my condition, either.

THOMAS. Come on, already.

> *(***THOMAS** *begins to exit the park.* **GEORGE** *follows.)*

GEORGE. Where's the love, I ask?

> *(***GEORGE** *begins singing in overly "soulful" tones.)*
>
> "Where's the love, you want to give me? Where's the love, I need some –
>
> *(in a bland announcer's voice)*
>
> Radio Edit."
>
> *(***GEORGE** *laughs.)*

THOMAS. *(shaking his head)* Dumb ass.

> *(Lights out.)*

Scene Four

(Lights up on the dining room/living room area of the house – a couple of days later. **JULIA** *is on the phone.)*

JULIA. Yes. No. More Options. *More Options.* Customer Service. Billing. Billing. *Billing.*

*(***THERESA*** enters and makes some tea.)*

Yes, hello, hi. I received a statement in the mail and I just wanted to make sure my ex-husband paid – no, no don't put me back to the…Yes. No. More Options. *More Options. Customer fucking Service.* Customer – useless.

*(***JULIA*** hangs up the phone. Tense quiet until…)*

THERESA. I could…

JULIA. No.

THERESA. The money from your father's insurance policy covers –

JULIA. *No.*

THERESA. It's not healthy, Julia. The credit card is in your name. He's never going to pay that bill in full which means it's just another reason for you to have contact with him.

JULIA. We raise a child together. It's not like this bill gets taken care of and we have no reason to communicate.

THERESA. I'm just trying to help.

JULIA. You do too much already.

THERESA. That's a mother's prerogative. I'd like to see you enjoy your life a little. You always seem to walk around the house in a state of continual discomfort.

JULIA. That's not true.

THERESA. It is true. You've been home for three years and you still seem so unsettled. If I can help eliminate some worry on your end, maybe you'll relax enough to have some fun for a change.

JULIA. Who's to say I haven't done that already?

*(***THERESA*** looks over to **JULIA**, suspiciously.)*

THERESA. Meaning?

(**JULIA** *smiles mischievously.*)

JULIA. Meaning, I have my first date next weekend.

THERESA. Julia, that's wonderful. Who is he?

JULIA. His name is David.

THERESA. David who?

JULIA. *(a bit apprehensive)* David Pearlstein.

THERESA. What a coincidence. I have a dentist named David Pearlstein.

JULIA. Yes, you do.

(**THERESA** *puts it together.*)

THERESA. Julia, are you going out on a date with my dentist?

JULIA. I am.

THERESA. *(immediately concerned)* You can't do that.

JULIA. Why not?

THERESA. It could end badly for me.

JULIA. What would any of it have to do with you?

THERESA. What if it doesn't work out? I'll have to change dentists. You know how hard it is to find someone of his caliber.

JULIA. You wouldn't have to leave.

THERESA. Of course I would, don't be naive. I couldn't have someone experiencing bad feelings for you while they had sharp instruments in my mouth.

JULIA. You're being dramatic.

THERESA. This is a drama. Of all the people, Julia, really.

JULIA. Mother.

THERESA. How did you even meet him?

JULIA. He called to confirm an appointment for you last month.

THERESA. Why did he call? He has a secretary. Lois. Very cranky woman with allergies. Where was she?

JULIA. Rehab.

THERESA. Oh.

JULIA. We met for coffee last week and now we've graduated to meals. Next weekend.

THERESA. He never said anything to me about it.

JULIA. We both agreed to keep it under wraps. Until now.

THERESA. *(not thrilled)* Congratulations.

JULIA. I thought you'd be happy.

THERESA. I am happy. It just seems so inappropriate.

JULIA. Get over it. He's cute and he's taking me to La Mesa.

THERESA. La Mesa. He must like you.

JULIA. You think so? He's not just being nice to a single mom?

THERESA. Burger Barn is being nice to a single Mom. He likes you.

(**THERESA** *looks to* **JULIA***, realizing…*)

He'll be the first one since Arthur. Things are civil between you and him?

JULIA. For the most part. Although, I really dug into him about his "three girls" philosophy the other day.

THERESA. Thomas is smarter than that.

JULIA. I hope so.

(**THERESA** *looks over to* **JULIA**.)

THERESA. He's going to keep asking about the divorce, you know?

JULIA. *(immediately tense)* Thanks for reminding me, Mother.

THERESA. He has a right to know.

JULIA. When he's older.

THERESA. But what does that mean, Julia? Every time you say older to him you might as well be saying you're never going to talk about it. That's how it feels to him.

JULIA. Mother.

THERESA. It's a part of his past. He'd like to know about it. I think that's fair. I mean, there are certain details about that subject I don't even know about. Hint, hint.

JULIA. You're going to gang up on me now?

THERESA. No one's ganging up on you.

JULIA. Who's side are you on?

THERESA. I'm on Thomas' side and you should be, too.

JULIA. I am on his side. It's just not time.

THERESA. Not time for him to know or not time for you to tell him? Is this about him or you?

JULIA. There's no great conspiracy against him. I'm not a bad mother.

THERESA. No one said you were.

JULIA. I understand his desire to know certain things, believe me.

THERESA. Then tell him.

JULIA. No.

THERESA. Julia.

(**JULIA**, *feeling overwhelmed, snaps.*)

JULIA. *No,* goddammit! Leave it alone!

(**THERESA** *backs down. Finally…*)

THERESA. No need for push-back.

JULIA. Then stop pushing.

THERESA. Pushing now ceased.

(*Lights out.*)

Scene Five

(Lights up on **THOMAS** *and* **ARTHUR** *at the park. It is the following Sunday. No food.* **ARTHUR** *is upset. In his hands is a cup of coffee.* **THOMAS** *has nothing.)*

ARTHUR. I can't believe you, T.

THOMAS. Sorry.

ARTHUR. Do you know how long I had to listen to your mother ream my "lowers" because you can't keep your mouth shut.

THOMAS. I didn't mean to –

ARTHUR. That was guy talk, T.

THOMAS. I know.

ARTHUR. Guy talk. I told you specifically, it was between the men. Do you listen?

THOMAS. I'm sorry.

ARTHUR. In one ear, out the *mother.* Sonofa…

*(**ARTHUR** trails off, shaking his head. He's very disappointed in his son. Finally after what seems like an eternity for* **THOMAS**, **ARTHUR** *looks over to him.)*

So…

*(**THOMAS** stares straight ahead.)*

You reading the newspaper these days? Staying informed on current events?

THOMAS. Yeah, I read the paper.

ARTHUR. Gotta stay informed.

THOMAS. I do.

ARTHUR. Good.

*(**ARTHUR** takes a sip of his coffee.)*

Which one? Which newspaper are you reading?

THOMAS. The "News."

ARTHUR. *(as if stung)* No, no, no. Don't read that one.

THOMAS. The other one's hard to fold.

ARTHUR. Doesn't matter. Stay away from the "News." All they do is complain about the government. It's misleading. Don't read it.

THOMAS. Okay.

ARTHUR. You can't read a lot of the newspapers now anyway because all they want to do is complain about the government. But the "News?" Get close enough to an election cycle and suddenly everything's wrong in the country, nothing works, we've become "Broken Town" – a product of the great conspiracy. But it's a lie. Things are never as bad as they say and their complaints always come at the expense of actual progress. We do a lot right in this country but you never hear about that.

THOMAS. Okay.

ARTHUR. You understand what I'm saying?

THOMAS. Yes, I think so.

ARTHUR. Good, 'cause you have to learn to read between the lies, find the truth for yourself. Don't accept what some flunky "journalist" tells you is the truth because the newspaper he whores for is run by some mega-corporation that told him to say it – it's not journalism, they're not journalists, they're pornographers in the corporate gang bang and you have to be ready to read it that way. It's like eating those grapes with the seeds in them.

THOMAS. Mom buys the seedless kind.

(**ARTHUR** *is immediately annoyed at the mention of* **JULIA.**)

ARTHUR. *(biting)* Well, isn't that convenient? How nice for you. Let me tell you something, Thomas. We'd all like to have the seedless grapes, just like we'd all like to have our news without lies but that's not how it works. This country, God Bless it, doesn't break things down that way. Truth is a specialty item here. So what are you going to do? Not eat grapes? Of course not. You're going to eat those grapes filled with seeds but you're not going to swallow the seeds either. You swallow too many of those seeds you get constipated. No, you separate the seeds from the pulp and you spit those goddamn seeds right out. That's how you have to learn to read the paper, Thomas. Because you have to read, you can't stay in the dark, there's no sadder place to be, let me tell you. But you can't swallow their lies, either. You have to learn how to separate the fact from fiction. So you can survive. You want to survive, don't you? You want to live?

THOMAS. Of course.

ARTHUR. This world moves fast, T. Things happen fast in it. Events. Discoveries. The only way to keep up with it, to ride safely in that slip stream, is by doing the right thing. Reading that paper the right way. But that takes strength. You have to be strong. Otherwise, all these events that happen will sweep you up and knock you around – you'll get knocked around regardless – but it'll be so bad you'll either die or you'll get so banged up you might as well be dead. Life isn't made for the weak, Thomas.

THOMAS. Okay.

ARTHUR. Nobody wants to be strong – strength is brutal, ugly, sometimes violent, even – but you have to be strong if you want to survive. So you read that goddamn paper like your life depends on it, because it does.

THOMAS. I see your point.

ARTHUR. Good.

(**ARTHUR** *looks at his watch.*)

Too late for a matinee now.

THOMAS. That's okay.

ARTHUR. You hungry? Want a hot dog or something? We got time for a dog. Or we could see what one of these squirrels taste like. You know in the south they call squirrels "tree chicken."

(**THOMAS** *does not respond. Finally…*)

ARTHUR. *(cont.)* That was a joke.

THOMAS. Yeah, no, that's okay. I'm not hungry.

(**ARTHUR** *looks at* **THOMAS**.)

ARTHUR. The "News."

(*Lights out.*)

Scene Six

(THERESA sits in a chair at the table doing a crossword puzzle. THOMAS sits on the floor doing his homework, wearing pajamas. JULIA is at the sink in the kitchen, washing a cup. It is later that night.)

THERESA. What's a seven letter word for "destructive?"

THOMAS. "Liberal?"

THERESA. Sweet boy.

THOMAS. You're welcome.

THERESA. *(writing)* I've got it. "Welfare."

(THERESA looks at the crossword, realizing that she's just more or less ruined it and puts the paper down.)

I just ruined my crossword.

THOMAS. "Theresa" has seven letters, too, you know.

THERESA. You have to sleep some time, Thomas.

THOMAS. I'll take my chances, Nana.

JULIA. Children.

(There's a knock at the door. Everyone stops what they're doing and looks up – this doesn't really happen much.)

Are you expecting someone?

THERESA. Not since the nineties, dear. Not since the nineties.

(THERESA walks over to the front door and opens it. On the other side of the door is CARLA RODRIGUEZ, the woman THOMAS was seeing. CARLA wears a business suit and is more than a little uncomfortable.)

THERESA. *(cont.)* May I help you?

CARLA. *(uncomfortable)* Yes, I was wondering if I may speak with Thomas.

THOMAS. Carla. Hi.

CARLA. Hello.

THERESA. You know this woman, Thomas?

(JULIA immediately moves to the door, realizing who it is.)

JULIA. *(stiff)* Yes, he does. Hi Carla. I'm Thomas' mother, Julia.

CARLA. Oh...hi.

JULIA. This is my mother, Theresa.

CARLA. Hello.

THERESA. Come right in, Carla.

(THERESA *closes the door behind* CARLA *as she awkwardly enters.* THOMAS, *by the look on his face, is happy to see her.*)

Would you like some tea, dear?

JULIA. That won't be necessary, Mom. Tea isn't a good idea right now.

THERESA. Since when is tea ever not a good idea?

CARLA. She's right, Theresa. It's okay. *Really.*

(*A pause in the room indicates a growing tension that* THERESA *doesn't understand until finally...*)

THERESA. *(confused)* What exactly am I missing?

JULIA. I didn't want to bother you with this.

THERESA. Bother me with what?

THOMAS. *(uncomfortable)* Theresa, Carla and I have history... together.

THERESA. *(to* CARLA*)* Aren't you a little old to be in history class with Thomas?

JULIA. He means actual history, mother.

THERESA. *(putting it together)* "Biblical history?"

CARLA. That's the one.

THERESA. Good Lord, how old are you?

CARLA. *(uncomfortable)* Thirty-two.

THERESA. Good Lord.

JULIA. Mother, calm down.

THERESA. Calm down? Thomas shouldn't even be having sex yet. I know I raised you with more values than this.

JULIA. Mother, please.

THERESA. He's fifteen years old.

THOMAS. I'll be sixteen.

THERESA. Did you think the catechism came with loop holes?

THOMAS. It's not her fault.

CARLA. It really isn't, Theresa.

> (**THERESA** *turns on* **CARLA**.)

THERESA. So you deflowered my daughter's fifteen year-old son?

THOMAS. *(defensive)* I wasn't a virgin.

CARLA. I did not know how old Thomas was at the time.

THOMAS. Yeah, I told her I was older and, besides there was this other girl at Space Camp who was my –

THERESA. *(interrupting)* Be that as it may, Carla, engaging in a sexual affair with someone you hardly know doesn't exactly seem responsible in this day and age.

CARLA. It happened very quickly but I assure you my intentions were good.

JULIA. It's not her fault either, Mom.

THOMAS. It's really not.

THERESA. *(exploding)* Well, it's somebody's fault!

THOMAS. If anyone's to blame it's me.

THERESA. Of course, blame the victim.

JULIA. Mother, she stopped seeing Thomas as soon as she found out his actual age. Sorry, Carla, please sit down.

CARLA. Thank you.

> (**CARLA** *sits down*.)

THERESA. May I get you something other than tea, dear? Pretzels? Beer? A small fifteen-year-old boy?

JULIA. Mother.

THOMAS. I'm not small.

JULIA. I'm sorry, Carla.

THOMAS. What about me?

CARLA. It's okay, I understand. I didn't plan on ever seeing your son again. When I found out how young he was, I was upset.

THOMAS. I apologized.

CARLA. I know.

> (awkward)

> So, how have you been?

THOMAS. Good. Yeah, I mean, you know...

CARLA. Good, I do, yes, sure...

> (They look at each other just long enough for JULIA to get uncomfortable.)

JULIA. So, Carla, what can we do for you?

CARLA. I'm finding myself in a bit of a situation and it seemed like I needed to find Thomas and speak with him about it.

JULIA. What could your situation possibly have to do with Thomas? I mean, what –

CARLA. I'm pregnant. I'm two months pregnant.

> (The information is a bombshell.)

> (No one knows quite what to say until without a word, THERESA stands and exits to the kitchen. After another beat, JULIA pushes THOMAS into his room and closes the door.)

THOMAS. Hey, hey, hey...

> (Beat. CARLA is alone until...JULIA reappears. She sits down without saying a word.)

> (THERESA comes out with the hot water and condiments.)

> (Finally...)

THERESA. Tea?

JULIA. So what are you going to do?

CARLA. I won't have an abortion.

THERESA. We're Republicans, dear.

JULIA. No one's asking you to have an abortion, Carla.

THERESA. Milk?

CARLA. No. I'm just putting it out there now so there's no misunderstanding. I'm going to keep this baby.

THERESA. You do realize you can't ask for better proof in a statutory rape case than evidence of the crime. Sugar?

CARLA. *No.* I didn't know Thomas was fifteen.

THOMAS. *(offstage)* I'll be sixteen.

JULIA. Thomas, stop listening through the door.

THOMAS. *(offstage)* I'm not listening through the door.

JULIA. Thomas!

THOMAS. I'm not. You're imagining it.

CARLA. He lied about his age. Everyone at this table is aware of that and Thomas has admitted as much. Besides, I still have Thomas' fake ID that he left at my apartment. I still have the voice mail messages of his where he apologized for lying about his age. This would all serve my "mistake of fact" defense. So the chances of me getting convicted are small in my estimation. I knew Thomas was young. Younger than me. But I had no idea he was that young and I'm sure I would be granted the benefit of the doubt if all of this had to see the light of day. That said, fifteen or no, Thomas can be legally made to honor any financial commitments he will have with this baby.

THERESA. Is that what this is? A shakedown? You've come into my home to shake us all down for money?

CARLA. If you're going to threaten jail, then, yes, that's exactly what this is.

THERESA. How dare you?

CARLA. How dare I? How dare you!

JULIA. Mom.

CARLA. I don't want money from either of you.

THERESA. Good, you won't be disappointed then when you don't get any.

CARLA. I've got money saved. I have a good job and my insurance is good. I'm here because I want Thomas and the both of you to know.

THERESA. Why?

CARLA. Because it's the right thing. One day Thomas will be an adult and on that day, I'm going to want a financial commitment from him then. Not you. Not now. Him. When he's of age.

(THOMAS *enters. He has changed out of his pajamas into very nice clothes.*)

JULIA. Thomas, what did I say?

THOMAS. I'm hearing my name.

JULIA. Go back to your room.

THOMAS. But you're talking about me.

JULIA. Go back to your room and take off your Sunday clothes.

THOMAS. You can't just send me to my room.

JULIA. Yes, I can.

THOMAS. I'm not a child, you know.

JULIA. You're fifteen years old.

THOMAS. I'll be sixteen, soon.

CARLA. He can be out here, Julia.

THERESA. I agree.

THOMAS. See that? You're the only one.

JULIA. Thank you, Mom.

THERESA. He needs to address this.

JULIA. No.

THERESA. Julia.

JULIA. Thomas, get back in your room! Now!

THOMAS. This sucks!

(THOMAS *slams the bedroom door shut.*)

JULIA. We have to figure out what we're going to do first.

THERESA. No door slamming, please.

(THOMAS *opens the bedroom door again.*)

THOMAS. You know something, I was man enough to start this problem, I think I'm man enough to be at the table to talk about it.

JULIA. Thomas.

THOMAS. Stop treating me like a child!

JULIA. You are a child.

THOMAS. *(stamping his feet)* I am not!

CARLA. Maybe he should be out here.

JULIA. Carla, nothing personal, but how I raise Thomas is not up for discussion by you.

THOMAS. Don't talk to her like that. She's the mother of my child.

JULIA. Oh, for heaven's sake.

THOMAS. That's my baby, too! She didn't do it by herself. I helped!

JULIA. Could we avoid those details for now?

THOMAS. I helped!

THERESA. Stop saying you helped. You made a baby, Thomas. You didn't "Shake and Bake."

JULIA. Thomas –

THOMAS. No, you're all talking about how I'm going to be responsible for it when I'm of legal age well then I'm going to be a part of this discussion.

JULIA. I'm losing my patience!

THOMAS. I'm standing right here! No one's going to make me go to my room. I don't do that anymore.

JULIA. Fine! Stay over there and listen but don't say anything.

*(This seems to calm **THOMAS** down for the moment and he stands there quietly listening. **JULIA** gathers herself and continues.)*

So what you're saying, Carla, is that you're going to have this baby and when Thomas is of legal age he's going to have to be financially responsible?

CARLA. Yes.

THOMAS. Will I get to spend time with it?

THERESA. "Its" not breaded chicken, Thomas. Don't refer to the baby as "it."

THOMAS. He/She. Will I?

CARLA. I don't know.

THOMAS. You don't know?

JULIA. Thomas.

THOMAS. No, I have to accept the financial burden but I won't get any of the benefits of being a father? Is that what you're saying?

CARLA. I'm saying you have a responsibility.

THOMAS. I have a right is what I have.

CARLA. Not necessarily.

THOMAS. Why? Because I lied to you? You're just getting back at me.

CARLA. I'm not getting back at you, Thomas.

THOMAS. That's what it seems like.

CARLA. It's not. I'm here telling you I'm pregnant, aren't I?

THOMAS. Only to rub it in my face.

CARLA. You think I wanted to get pregnant?

THOMAS. Maybe.

CARLA. Excuse me?

THOMAS. No, I don't think I will. I went online and found out how unreliable cervical caps are as contraception.

JULIA. When were you online?

THOMAS. When you sent me to my room. I went on the computer.

THERESA. *(to JULIA)* Devil's Highway.

THOMAS. You're a smart lady, Carla, what are you doing using contraception with that kind of a failure rate?

CARLA. I did not want to get pregnant.

THOMAS. You might as well have been playing Russian Roulette with my penis.

JULIA. Thomas, stop. You're over-reacting.

THOMAS. No, actually I'm being told, once again, to act like an adult but whenever I say grown up things that anyone here doesn't like, I hear, "Be quiet. Stop overreacting. You're just a kid." Well, I won't be both because it's convenient for you. I'm sick of it. I'm just sick of it.

CARLA. There's nothing convenient about any of this for me.

THOMAS. I want to see my baby when He/She's born. I want Her/Him to know I'm the father.

CARLA. I don't know if that will ever be possible.

THOMAS. Once I'm eighteen, you won't have a choice! You're a lawyer, you know that!

JULIA. Thomas!

THOMAS. I can see Him/Her on Sundays if I want!

JULIA. Thomas, stop!

THOMAS. No, I can! I can take He/She to the park! We can go to the movies and eat hot dogs and you can't stop me!

JULIA. Calm down!

THOMAS. *(exploding with fury)* Stop telling me to calm down! Stop telling me I'm over-reacting! I won't calm down and I'll react however the hell I want to react! You don't do that! No one does that!

JULIA. What has gotten into you?

THOMAS. Are you that out of it?

JULIA. Answer the question.

THOMAS. You! You've gotten into me! And you, Theresa and you, Carla. All of you've gotten into me so if you don't like it, well, tough because that's the way it is and it's all your fault and I'm not going to feel bad or embarrassed about it anymore! In fact, the hell with this standing, I'm going to sit down at this table now.

(**THOMAS** *sits down at the table and folds his arms.*)

JULIA. Here we go.

THERESA. Would you like some tea, Captain Grown-Up?

THOMAS. No, I'm here to talk. Let's talk, let's go.

CARLA. Thomas, you can think what you like, but I came here because I felt it was the right thing to tell you what was going on but that doesn't mean you have a right to –

THOMAS. You're wrong.

CARLA. I'm not.

THOMAS. We'll see about that.

CARLA. What are you going to do, Thomas?

THOMAS. Well, for one thing, I'm not going to my room. I'm staying right here and I'm going to be a father and support our baby.

THERESA. With what money?

JULIA. She's right. How are you going to pay for this child? We're still paying for you now.

THOMAS. I'll get a job.

JULIA. Doing what?

THOMAS. Whatever I have to do. What difference does it make?

JULIA. It makes all the difference! What about college? What about doing something with your life?

THOMAS. This looks like something to me. Raising a child is something. That's what you did.

JULIA. You're too young to have a child! You are a child!

THOMAS. That didn't stop you! You were right out of high school! Isn't that how it happened?

JULIA. That was different!

THOMAS. You were barely graduated when you got pregnant with me.

JULIA. I was an adult!

THOMAS. Two years does not an adult make!

THERESA. Three years is the actual number for you.

THOMAS. Oh, well, two years and three months if you're going to be like that, Granny.

JULIA. I will not listen to this nonsense.

THOMAS. You're such a hypocrite!

JULIA. I will not watch you throw away your life.

THOMAS. Then close your eyes! It's how you handle everything else!

JULIA. You don't know what you're getting yourself into!

THOMAS. I'll learn!

JULIA. It's not an education you want!

THOMAS. Don't give me that! You had me young!

JULIA. *(exploding)* And look how well it turned out for me, you little shit!

(**THOMAS** *is stung by this.*)

(**THOMAS** *gets up from the table. He looks to* **CARLA**, *back to his mother and walks out of the house. No one is sure what to say.*)

(Lights out.)

Scene Seven

(Lights up on **THOMAS** *and* **ARTHUR**. *It is the following Sunday – a week after* **CARLA**'s *revelation.* **THOMAS**
*wears a blank expression. There's a hot dog in his hand
but he hasn't eaten any of it.* **ARTHUR** *has a cup of
coffee, he sips at it.)*

ARTHUR. Are you sure?

THOMAS. Yes.

ARTHUR. No question it's yours?

THOMAS. No question.

ARTHUR. Well, then I hate to say I told you so. But I told
you so, you dummy. She's got you by the DNA now,
you're screwed.

THOMAS. Yes sir.

ARTHUR. Get very comfortable with the term "garnished
wages" 'cause that little money magnet just found the
mother vein. I told you it was a mistake to put your
cock in that, Thomas.

THOMAS. You did tell me after the fact.

ARTHUR. Boo-hoo, oh well, life's forever. You going to cry
about it?

THOMAS. No, I'm not going to cry.

ARTHUR. What are you going to do, then? Now that you are
a statistical blemish, what are your plans?

THOMAS. I don't know.

ARTHUR. Wrong. Not an answer. What are you going to do,
Thomas?

THOMAS. I was thinking about getting a job, maybe.

ARTHUR. A job? What the hell would you do that for? So
she can take everything you earn? You don't need a
wage she can draw from right now.

THOMAS. She wouldn't be taking it for herself. It would be
for the baby.

ARTHUR. Don't be surprised if baby needs a new pair of
Manolo Blahniks.

THOMAS. A new pair of what?

ARTHUR. Forget it. And forget about a job. You want to do something smart? Stay in school. Period. High School. College. Graduate School. Doctorate Program. You want to learn how to weld after that, knock yourself cross-eyed. Stay in those places because it sucks out here in the real world, trust me. Stay in school. Much safer. You ever notice how they don't have a "No Child Left Behind" Law outside of school? Case closed.

THOMAS. By the time I'm legal, Carla is going to want me to start paying for the baby.

ARTHUR. Getting a job now isn't going to be the answer.

THOMAS. What is?

ARTHUR. Filing charges for sexual assault.

THOMAS. But she didn't sexually assault me.

ARTHUR. You're a minor. She sexually assaulted you.

THOMAS. But I lied to her.

ARTHUR. So lie some more. Only now, instead of lying to get laid, you can lie to get some cover.

THOMAS. Too many people know, already. Besides, even if I lie to get her in trouble, I'll still have to help pay for the baby but now if she's in jail, I'll be on my own with him/her.

ARTHUR. Well, you don't want that brain tumor.

THOMAS. I guess not.

ARTHUR. Nothing to guess about, believe me. Having a kid at your age is the last thing you need.

THOMAS. Mom was almost my age when she had me.

(Silence. Finally…)

She said having me was a bad thing.

ARTHUR. *(amused)* She said that? Geez, I guess being single has been hard on her. Bitter.

*(**ARTHUR** looks at **THOMAS** who seems to be somewhere else.)*

You don't talk to your Mother about important stuff like that, huh? Her dating habits?

(**THOMAS** *doesn't respond. Finally...*)

ARTHUR. *(cont.)* It's okay not to talk to your mother about everything. Some things you can't explain to her and you shouldn't. You can always talk to me, though. I mean, your bedroom's always there, exactly how you left it, if you ever need it, you know? Anything you want to talk about...anything...you can talk to me. Yeah? Okay?

THOMAS. Okay.

ARTHUR. Okay?

THOMAS. Sure.

ARTHUR. Good.

THOMAS. Why did you two divorce?

ARTHUR. *(nervous)* Oh, well, listen, T, you have more important things –

THOMAS. No, you want to talk to me about something, talk to me about that. This conversation's overdue.

ARTHUR. But that's not –

THOMAS. Tell me.

ARTHUR. There's nothing about that that's useful –

THOMAS. Help me out or I'm walking.

ARTHUR. *(menacing)* What did you just say to me, young man?

THOMAS. All you do is talk to me about crap I could care less about.

ARTHUR. Excuse me for trying to teach you something.

THOMAS. You really want to teach me something? Tell me why you divorced.

ARTHUR. Ask your mother.

THOMAS. She won't tell me.

ARTHUR. Then I can't help you. I promised her I wouldn't say anything.

THOMAS. Tell me or you can forget Sundays.

ARTHUR. Don't you threaten me, you little punk.

THOMAS. If you loved me, you would tell me.

ARTHUR. Why? Why, with everything else going on with you, is it so goddamn important now?

THOMAS. I am in a situation with this woman and I need to know things about myself – anything – that might help me sort it out. I need to sort.

ARTHUR. Sort?

THOMAS. When I'm in school and I have to study for a test in a class that I spent the last few months zoning out in, I put all the information in front of me and sort through it all and that helps prepare me. It helps me understand what I'm walking into.

ARTHUR. Life ain't high school, T.

THOMAS. I need to sort, Dad. Can you just let me sort? Why won't you let me sort?

ARTHUR. What the fuck is sorting? What the fuck are you talking about?

THOMAS. Sorting helps me understand. Me. My situation. You. Mom.

ARTHUR. Why we divorced won't help your…"sorting."

THOMAS. Then it's wasted time, "boo-hoo, oh well, life's forever."

ARTHUR. Don't you mock me.

THOMAS. I need to know this and you're the only one who can help me.

ARTHUR. It won't help you. Trust me, Thomas.

THOMAS. I'm not trusting anyone on this anymore.

ARTHUR. Well, you're gonna have to because you have enough to think about without strolling down Memory Pain.

THOMAS. Tell me!

ARTHUR. Forget it, Thomas.

THOMAS. Help me sort!

ARTHUR. Stop pushing me!

THOMAS. I want to know, goddammit!

ARTHUR. Back the fuck off, right the fuck now, young man!

THOMAS. Tell me what you know!

ARTHUR. I'm warning you!

THOMAS. Why did you two divorce?

ARTHUR. No!

THOMAS. Tell me or fuck you!

ARTHUR. *(exploding)* I'm not your biological father! None of my blood is in you! There, you happy, tough guy? Sort through that, you little shit! Your mother got pregnant and tricked me into marrying her! Welcome to the real world, Thomas! I'm a fool and you're a bastard!

(**THOMAS** *is stunned. The two stare at each other, as if for the first time.*)

(Lights out.)

End of Act One

ACT TWO

Scene One

(Lights up. **THERESA** *sits at the dining room table in the living room. It's late – about 1:00am. Only one light seems to illuminate the stage. After a moment, the sound of keys is heard in the door.* **JULIA** *enters. She wears a nice dress and is a little tipsy.* **JULIA** *closes the door and quietly locks it, thinking she is alone until...)*

THERESA. Hello there, night owl.

JULIA. *(startled)* Oh, Mother. I didn't see you.

THERESA. Did you have a good time with Dr. Pearlstein?

JULIA. *(giggling)* I had a wonderful time with the good dentist, thank you very much.

THERESA. I'm glad.

(beat)

JULIA. Is Thomas home?

THERESA. He's been asleep for a few hours.

JULIA. Good, good.

THERESA. "Good" is not exactly the word I would use to describe him of late.

*(***JULIA*** *begins adjusting her belt.)*

JULIA. *(not listening)* No?

THERESA. No, he's a little confused these days, I think. Carla. The divorce. You telling him his birth was a burden.

JULIA. Oh, that's not what...I was angry...

THERESA. I believe the words "little shit" were used.

JULIA. I've apologized to him for that. I'll apologize again if I have to.

THERESA. He's been moping around. You may have to.

JULIA. *(annoyed)* Fine. I will. Anything else, joy kill?

THERESA. He's gotten himself a job.

JULIA. What? Where?

THERESA. He was hiding his little uniform but I spied a part of it as he came in tonight. Seems he's doing a little "fast food maintenance" at the Burger Barn.

JULIA. What is that boy up to?

THERESA. He hasn't been speaking much to me but if I had to guess, I would say it looks like he's attempting to be a provider.

JULIA. You think he's giving his money to Carla?

THERESA. If I had to guess.

JULIA. I'll speak with him tomorrow. Too late now.

THERESA. That it is.

(**JULIA** *takes a moment, realizing* **THERESA** *is still awake at such a late hour.*)

JULIA. What are you still doing up?

THERESA. When you first moved back in, I wasn't used to people in the house. Now I'm not used to feeling so alone.

JULIA. I should've called.

THERESA. Your father and I managed to get through all those years without ever seeing you and Thomas. I can manage a few hours now.

JULIA. I'm sorry.

THERESA. For which part? Tonight or the twelve years when you wouldn't return my phone calls?

JULIA. What is this?

THERESA. This is me thinking out loud.

JULIA. About what?

THERESA. Why you really stayed away for so long.

JULIA. I told you, Arthur didn't want me to see you guys – he was very controlling.

THERESA. He barely knew us. You barely knew him. Why would he do that?

JULIA. You'll have to ask him.

THERESA. I'd rather hear it from you.

JULIA. I thought we were past this.

THERESA. Were you ashamed, Julia?

JULIA. What? *No.*

THERESA. I'd just like to know.

JULIA. I wasn't ashamed.

THERESA. I could understand if you were. Arthur not being the biological father. Having to lie to him and Thomas. I know that must have been hard but why did you shut your father and me out?

JULIA. I'm back now.

THERESA. Where else were you going to go once Arthur discovered the truth and threw you out?

JULIA. That's not fair.

THERESA. Your life is unraveled by a blood test and you call me as though it had only been a few days since we'd seen each other last. You want to talk about fair?

JULIA. Mother –

THERESA. Did we do something wrong?

JULIA. No, nothing.

THERESA. Your father never had a chance to even know Thomas existed.

JULIA. Look, I just had a very nice evening – the first real nice evening in awhile.

THERESA. Oh, I'm sorry. Am I ruining your night?

JULIA. Actually, yes.

THERESA. Why did you shut us out?

JULIA. Stop.

THERESA. Do you even know who the real father is, Julia?

JULIA. *(snapping)* Stop it, stop it, stop it!

THERESA. No I won't!

*(**THOMAS** enters fully dressed with a bag. He has a detached look to him.)*

THERESA. *(cont.)* Thomas, I thought you were asleep.

JULIA. Did we wake you?

THOMAS. No.

THERESA. Is everything okay?

THOMAS. No.

JULIA. What are you doing with that bag?

THOMAS. I'm moving out.

JULIA. What did you say?

THOMAS. I'm moving in with Arthur.

(Stares all around.)

(Lights out.)

Scene Two

(Lights up on the park. It is the next day. **ARTHUR** *sits on the bench, waiting.* **JULIA** *appears.)*

JULIA. Arthur.

*(***ARTHUR** *immediately stands up.)*

ARTHUR. Julia.

(For a brief moment they just stand there. Finally…)

So…

JULIA. Why did you tell him?

ARTHUR. He had a right to know.

JULIA. We agreed to wait.

ARTHUR. You agreed. I just went along.

JULIA. If you were going along, why did you tell him?

ARTHUR. He kept pushing me.

JULIA. That doesn't mean you had to tell him.

ARTHUR. Maybe I got tired of being the bad guy. Maybe I got tired of lying to the boy. Maybe it's time some dirt rubbed off on you.

JULIA. He won't talk to me.

ARTHUR. He's mad at you.

*(***ARTHUR** *notices how much this upsets* **JULIA** *and he softens just a bit.)*

He doesn't say much to me either, Jules. Just so you know.

(beat)

JULIA. How is he?

ARTHUR. He's taking it hard.

*(***JULIA** *nods.)*

He keeps asking me who his biological father is.

JULIA. *(tense)* What do you tell him?

ARTHUR. I tell him I don't know. Against my better judgement, I lie.

JULIA. Thank you.

ARTHUR. You're welcome.

   (beat)

ARTHUR. *(cont.)* Do you want to sit down?

JULIA. *(checking her watch)* No, Mom's waiting in the car. I have to drop her off at Botox.

ARTHUR. Botox?

JULIA. Yes.

ARTHUR. What's she getting all smoothed out for?

JULIA. It doesn't matter. I have to take her. Plus, I have another…appointment.

ARTHUR. With Dr. Pearlstein?

JULIA. How do you…?

ARTHUR. The boy's living in my house now, Julia. He talks, he tells me things.

JULIA. He shouldn't have.

ARTHUR. He's a dentist, this guy?

JULIA. Arthur.

ARTHUR. Just making small talk.

JULIA. No, you're making fires.

ARTHUR. Okay, okay.

JULIA. I'm here about Thomas.

THOMAS. You're here to rag me about Thomas.

JULIA. I'm worried about him.

ARTHUR. Hey, I'm worried, too. He's living in my house for God's sake. I'm helping him out. I'm helping you, too.

JULIA. You're helping him?

ARTHUR. Yes, I am, goddamn it!

JULIA. Like the "three girls and some spooge" theory that you laid on him? That's the kind of help you're talking about?

ARTHUR. You're going to ream me about that again?

JULIA. *(overlapping)* You are teaching him to disrespect women, Arthur…

ARTHUR. *(overlapping)* Here we go. I am not. That's not true…

JULIA. *(overlapping)* You are teaching him to treat some women like garbage…like they're trash…

ARTHUR. *(overlapping)* I am doing no such thing. Get the hell out of here with…that's a lie…

JULIA. *(overlapping)* You most certainly are. Ectoplasmic… crude, repugnant…is what you are…you really are, Arthur…

ARTHUR. *(overlapping)* Crude and repugnant would have been letting him think he loved that little Puerto Rican child molester…

JULIA. *(overlapping)* This is exactly what I'm talking about!

ARTHUR. *(overlapping)* I'm trying…

JULIA. *(overlapping)* You're making it worse…

ARTHUR. *(overlapping)* I'm making sure he doesn't find himself married before he even graduates.

JULIA. *(overlapping)* You're being ridiculous! Absolutely absurd!

ARTHUR. *(overlapping)* I'm being a parent! You should try it some time!

(The argument spends itself. They both stand there, breathing heavily. Finally…)

JULIA. Does everything have to be difficult with you?

ARTHUR. I'm the one that was lied into this. I'm the one who woke up one morning to find out the joke was on him and I've been picking up the slack ever since. Keeping the lie together. Doing all the PR for you – Mom of the Year.

(For a moment nothing is spoken. Until…)

This dentist you're seeing? He's Jewish, right?

JULIA. I'm leaving.

ARTHUR. Don't you think that might confuse Thomas if everything is suddenly a wailing wall of Hebrew?

JULIA. I hardly think any of that is your business.

ARTHUR. I just don't want the boy to be any more confused than he already is.

JULIA. Will you work with me on this? Will you work with me to help him through this.

ARTHUR. What kind of question is that?

JULIA. It's my question. Will you?

ARTHUR. Of course, I'll work with you.

JULIA. Thank you.

> *(pause)*
>
> *(In the background, a gunshot is heard.* **ARTHUR** *does not pay it much attention but* **JULIA** *does.)*

ARTHUR. See? It doesn't all have to be ass-y.

JULIA. *(looking around)* Arthur.

ARTHUR. *(not listening)* I know, I know, Jules…I get cranky. I hear stories about you going out on dates and it makes me…

JULIA. *(not listening)* This is where you and Thomas spend your Sundays?

ARTHUR. *(not listening)* A part of me still resents how –

JULIA. This place, Arthur.

ARTHUR. What? What about it?

JULIA. You take Thomas here on Sundays?

ARTHUR. Every Sunday, sure. It's nice. So?

JULIA. I just heard gunfire.

ARTHUR. The park is fine.

JULIA. It sounds dangerous.

ARTHUR. I grew up in this park.

JULIA. What if something happens?

ARTHUR. Nothing will happen.

JULIA. I just heard gunfire.

ARTHUR. *(overlapping)* Oh for…it's always the same with you. You're relentless.

JULIA. *(overlapping)* It's always the same because you never change.

ARTHUR. *(overlapping)* You go on and on. You never stop.

JULIA. *(overlapping)* You never think of what your actions mean for other people. You carry on, you act out…

ARTHUR. *(overlapping)* Isn't this the pot calling the kettle…

JULIA. *(overlapping)* You're just a bitter mess.

ARTHUR. *(overlapping)* I concede on one thing just to make things easier…

JULIA. *(overlapping)* Just a bitter, hopeless mess of…

ARTHUR. *(overlapping)* …and instead of you appreciating that, which you never do…

JULIA. *(overlapping)* …ugliness and resentment…

ARTHUR. *(overlapping)* …all you want to do is use that newly gained ground to push a little more.

JULIA. *(overlapping)* You can't let anything go.

ARTHUR. *(overlapping)* Projecting back to me like I'm the messed up one.

JULIA. *(overlapping)* You have hold onto it and let it fester there.

ARTHUR. Like I'm the one who needs fixing.

JULIA. *(overlapping)* Because you're broken!

ARTHUR. *(exploding and topping)* And you did it! It's your fault! My marriage! My trust! I'm the one who was conned! I'm the one who took Thomas to the Emergency Room when he wrecked his bike! I'm the one who offered himself up for a blood transfusion only to discover, I wasn't a match! I'm the one who had to live through that moment! Not you! Me! Alone! And instead of appreciating, understanding, sympathizing, all you do is try to find things about me that are wrong or awful so that you don't feel like such a bad person! Like it makes what you did not so bad and you hold onto it and visit it and re-visit it and it's sick, Julia – but you are wrong! You still are!

(Beat. Until…)

JULIA. *(checking her watch)* I have to go.

ARTHUR. So, go.

JULIA. Can you at least pretend we're working together on this?

ARTHUR. Can you at least pretend you ever had a feeling for me? That I wasn't just convenient.

JULIA. That's not fair.

(**ARTHUR** *jumps to his feet.*)

ARTHUR. Good! Now you know how I feel! Look at us, Jules! At last. The two of us on the same page – no – on the same line on the same page. We can finish each other's sentences. That's how aligned we are now. Hallelujah.

(*Beat. Then…*)

Don't worry about Thomas. I'll take care of him.

JULIA. It's only temporary, you know? Thomas staying with you.

ARTHUR. I wouldn't push that boy to make a decision right now because we both know which way he's leaning. He's in good hands for now; leave it at that.

JULIA. Fine.

(**JULIA** *moves to exit.*)

ARTHUR. Julia.

(**JULIA** *stops and turns back to* **ARTHUR**.)

JULIA. What, Arthur?

ARTHUR. Thomas will have to know at some point.

JULIA. No one has to know.

ARTHUR. Something like that…it's not fair to him.

JULIA. Don't you tell him.

ARTHUR. Why? Because he'd really hate you, then? Because then he'd know how you must really feel about him?

JULIA. Don't you do it, Arthur.

ARTHUR. I may have to, Julia.

JULIA. Don't you do something like that just to get back at me.

ARTHUR. I'd be doing it for the boy, Julia. Not you.

JULIA. *(real menace)* Arthur, I swear to God if you tell him, I'll…

(**JULIA** *stops herself. Finally…*)

I have to go.

ARTHUR. So, go.

JULIA. And pay your credit card bill. They're sending me threats in the mail again.

ARTHUR. Fine.

(**JULIA** *exits.* **ARTHUR** *is alone.*)

Fine.

(Lights out.)

Scene Three

(Lights up. It is later in the afternoon. **CARLA** *stands at a bus stop.* **THOMAS** *suddenly appears and approaches.* **THOMAS** *is dressed up in very nice clothes.)*

THOMAS. Carla.

CARLA. Thomas, what are you doing?

THOMAS. I wanted to see you.

CARLA. When we broke up and I said I didn't think we should see each other, I meant it. This development doesn't change a thing.

THOMAS. I know that. I know what you said.

CARLA. So?

THOMAS. I think what you're doing is selfish.

CARLA. It's what I have to do.

THOMAS. But it's selfish.

CARLA. Then it's selfish.

THOMAS. Fine, then I'm going to be selfish, too. I'll be selfish and see you when you don't want me to.

CARLA. Why do you want to see me, Thomas?

*(***THOMAS*** reaches into his pocket and takes out some money.)*

THOMAS. Here.

CARLA. What is that?

THOMAS. I've been working. I got paid.

CARLA. I don't want your money now, Thomas.

THOMAS. Take it!

CARLA. No!

*(***THOMAS*** throws the money at her, violently.)*

THOMAS. Fuck you, then!

CARLA. Yeah? Well, fuck you, too! Fuck you for doing this to me!

THOMAS. How many times do I have to apologize for that?

CARLA. It's not about apologizing!

THOMAS. Then what is it about? Tell me.

CARLA. You wouldn't understand. You're just part of the problem.

THOMAS. I want to fix it!

CARLA. You can't. You lied to me. That's never going to be fixed. You can't go back and do that over! This is going to stay with you! Always!

THOMAS. You don't want this baby. You're just doing it to stick it to me.

CARLA. This is not about you anymore! This is about me now and I don't have any other choice!

THOMAS. You could have an abortion.

CARLA. Fuck you! I'm not living with that! Having this baby is the last thing I need to do but I'm going to it and when the baby's old enough to ask questions, I'm going to tell him or her all about you and it won't be kind, it'll be the truth and I swear I'll make sure they'll hate you for it! Just like I hate you for it!

THOMAS. That doesn't make any sense.

CARLA. *(withering)* You're just a boy, Thomas.

THOMAS. You didn't think that when I was inside of you.

(*CARLA slaps* **THOMAS**. **THOMAS**, *on instinct, slaps her back.* **CARLA** *tries to run from* **THOMAS** *but he grabs her by the wrist.*)

CARLA. Let me go.

THOMAS. No, I won't.

CARLA. You're hurting me.

THOMAS. Good. Pain's appropriate.

CARLA. Help! Someone help me! Help!!

(**THOMAS** *puts his hand over* **CARLA**'s *mouth, covering it.*)

THOMAS. *(violent)* Shut up! Shut, shut up, shut up!

(*She stops screaming. After a moment,* **THOMAS** *uncovers her mouth and releases her hand. The two stand there, saying nothing, breathing heavily.*)

(Finally, **CARLA** *and* **THOMAS** *begin kissing and groping passionately until* **CARLA** *breaks away from* **THOMAS** *.)*

THOMAS. *(cont.)* Carla.

*(***CARLA** *walks away from* **THOMAS** *and the bus stop, almost in a daze.* **THOMAS** *follows her offstage.)*

(Lights out.)

Scene Four

*(Lights up. **THERESA** reads a newspaper while **JULIA***
*folds some of **THOMAS'** clothes. It is later that night.*
***THERESA** is sporting a very small but noticeable black*
eye. The quiet in the room is unnerving for both of them.
Finally...)

JULIA. How's the eye?

THERESA. Sore. How does it look?

JULIA. It looks sore. And black. Black and sore.

THERESA. I shouldn't have moved while Dr. Thompson was injecting me.

JULIA. It'll fade soon enough.

THERESA. It's actually kind of fun, if you want to know the truth.

JULIA. Your black eye is fun?

THERESA. I admit there is a certain level of discomfort. But the man from the post office was convinced my husband was abusing me. He told me, "Darling, a beautiful woman like yourself shouldn't have to put up with a man who treats you that way." And I smiled bashfully, giving him a warm, silent look of gratitude before timidly leaving that post office with the comforting glow of a woman who knows somewhere, someone out there thinks I still have a man in my life.

JULIA. You've outdone the shower head, mother.

THERESA. I'm not making light of domestic violence.

JULIA. *(sarcastic)* Of course not. No one would think that.

THERESA. I'm just saying it felt nice to be thought of as someone who wasn't alone.

JULIA. *(defensive)* You're not alone. You have me. And Thomas. Well, we'll both have Thomas again, soon.

THERESA. It's quiet without him around here.

JULIA. It really is.

(slight pause)

THERESA. It was even quieter when your father died.

JULIA. Mom.

THERESA. All of it was quiet as I remember now. Even the preamble to all that quiet was "low decibel" in nature. Of course, you weren't around for that. His illness. His hospice. His death. You missed all of those things. You made it to the funeral, though, so I suppose one out of four isn't bad. Or is it two out of three isn't bad? Yes, I think that's right. One out of four is actually awful.

(Beat. Then...)

JULIA. I'm sorry.

*(**THERESA** takes a moment, considering something, until...)*

THERESA. This is becoming a real sticking point with me, Julia.

JULIA. I'm noticing.

THERESA. Am I not old enough to handle the truth, dear?

JULIA. There's no –

THERESA. *(mocking)* Shall we wait another few years before you think I'm ready?

JULIA. It's not that. It's –

(Suddenly, there is a pounding on the door.)

What the...?

THOMAS. *(off-stage)* Open the door! Open up.

JULIA. Thomas? Is that you?

THOMAS. *(off-stage)* Open it up! I want to talk to you!

*(**JULIA** moves to the door and opens up the door revealing a very drunk **THOMAS**. **THOMAS** barges past his mother and into the house.)*

JULIA. What is going...?

THOMAS. I want to know a few things now, please, thank you!

THERESA. He's drunk.

JULIA. You think?

THOMAS. I would like to know some things!

JULIA. Thomas, settle down.

THOMAS. I can't. I've had too much Scotch.

THERESA. Where did you get the Scotch?

JULIA. I can only imagine.

THOMAS. Imagine an answer for me somewhere in that imagination of yours. Imaginatively.

JULIA. Did something happen?

THOMAS. Yes! Yes, something happened, you crazy lady! I just found out my father isn't my father. And yet I'm still living in his house in what used to be my bedroom. Which, by the way, he has preserved like a museum. That man hasn't changed a thing. It is beyond creepy and I actually have had enough distance to realize a few things.

JULIA. Thomas –

THOMAS. Were you aware I had a Nickelback poster on my wall?

THERESA. What's a Nickelback?

JULIA. They're a rock band, I think.

THOMAS. Nickelback!

THERESA. I'll get him some water.

(THERESA *goes into the kitchen.*)

THOMAS. You must have known that was a bad idea, right? I mean, culturally speaking, you could've helped me out on the Nickelback poster.

JULIA. You're not making any sense.

THOMAS. I make all the sense I need to.

JULIA. That does –

THOMAS. Who's my Bio-D?

JULIA. Who's your what?

THOMAS. My biological daddy! Who's my daddy, mommy?

(THOMAS *starts laughing and coughing.*)

That's funny. Who's my daddy?

(THERESA *comes out with a glass of water and hands it to* THOMAS *who takes the glass and begins gesticulating wildly with it, spilling it's contents everywhere.*)

Who's my daddy?

(THERESA, *very patiently grabs the glass from* THOMAS.)

THERESA. I'll get you some more water and a towel.

JULIA. Don't use a glass one this time, Mom.

THERESA. Check.

JULIA. There should be some paper ones in the basement.

THERESA. I'll go look.

THOMAS. Yeah, keep me away from the sharp things. Don't want me to hurt myself. That's your job.

(**THERESA** *exits into the kitchen.*)

JULIA. Thomas, please.

THOMAS. Who is he?

JULIA. Thomas.

THOMAS. No. Who's my father?

(**ARTHUR** *comes through the door.*)

ARTHUR. Thomas. What the hell are you doing?

THOMAS. Hello, Arthur. I see you remember where I used to live. Would you like to see my old room. Not as nice as my original room but it is "Nickelback free."

ARTHUR. *(to* **JULIA***)* He's been at my Scotch.

JULIA. Really? Genius, Art.

THOMAS. Art, right. You call him, Art. Arty. Hey Arty. What's up, Arty? Art-e.

(*He starts laughing some more.*)

ARTHUR. I'll get him home and sober.

THOMAS. No sober. I'm not leaving until you tell me who he is.

JULIA. Thomas.

THOMAS. Nope. I want a name. Someone with a phone number, you lying little thing. You're just a thing until then, okay? Until, I get some truth from you, you're just a *thing.*

JULIA. Thomas.

THOMAS. Who's my father, *thing?*

JULIA. You're drunk!

THOMAS. Thank you for stating the obvious. We now return to our regularly scheduled program.

JULIA. This is not the right time.

THOMAS. Too bad, *thing-e*! Let it spill! Come on, give it to me!

ARTHUR. Maybe he should know, Jules.

JULIA. Arthur, goddammit, don't you dare get involved in this.

ARTHUR. I am involved in this.

THOMAS. You know who he is, Art?

ARTHUR. Yes, I do.

JULIA. Think about this for a moment. Think about where we are.

ARTHUR. There's never going to be perfect time.

THOMAS. He's right, *thing-face*. The timing will always suck.

JULIA. Don't do this to me!

ARTHUR. This isn't about you.

JULIA. It isn't about you, either!

THOMAS. Don't listen to her! She's just mad! She's got woman baggage. Right, Art? You know what I'm talking about. Right?

JULIA. Don't!

THOMAS. Hey, is he a priest?

ARTHUR. He's going to find out sooner or later.

THOMAS. Porn star?

JULIA. That does not have to translate to tonight!

THOMAS. He's not one of the guys from Nickelback, is he?

JULIA. Don't do this, Arthur!

THOMAS. Tell me, already!

ARTHUR. Your father is *her* father.

(**THOMAS** *takes a stunned moment to try and process this until...*)

THOMAS. Wait...does that even make sense? I mean...what does that even...I mean, technically speaking...

ARTHUR. Technically speaking, it means your mother is also your sister. Half. Technically.

(**THOMAS** *just stands there absorbing until...*)

JULIA. Sonofabitch! You Sonofabitch!

*(**JULIA** lunges at **ARTHUR** with violent intentions. She attempts several times to strike him but **ARTHUR** deflects her.)*

*(Suddenly, **THOMAS**, flies into a rage. He attacks **ARTHUR** and **JULIA**, throwing them both to the ground.)*

THOMAS. *(exploding)* You dirty fucking liars! All this time!

*(**THOMAS** begins knocking over pictures, some of them, pictures of the grandfather, Samuel. Behind the pictures, the wallpaper appears discolored from age.)*

Selfish and ugly and vicious and hateful and you turn all of that on me! A fucking crime! I'm a fucking crime! Fuck you! Fuck me! Fuck it all, cause it's done! All of it, all of this is done!

*(**THOMAS** spends himself, collapsing into a nearby chair.)*

I'm done.

*(Pause as both **JULIA** and **ARTHUR** try to process **THOMAS**'s outburst.)*

JULIA. Are you okay, Thomas?

*(**THOMAS** looks over at his mother like she's crazy.)*

JULIA. *(cont.)* I mean, are you feeling…

ARTHUR. You look a little pale.

*(**THOMAS** sits there in the chair not responding.)*

JULIA. Thomas?

THOMAS. I think…

ARTHUR. Yes?

THOMAS. I think…I'm sober.

JULIA. You're sober?

THOMAS. No.

ARTHUR. No?

THOMAS. No, I think I'm going to be sick.

*(**THOMAS** clasps his hand over his mouth, leaping out of the chair.)*

ARTHUR. Okay. It's okay, Thomas. I'll take care of you.

JULIA. You sonofabitch.

(**ARTHUR** *moves to* **THOMAS**, *protective, possessive even. He glares sullenly at* **JULIA**.)

ARTHUR. At least, I'd never put my kid through what you did.

THOMAS. I'm really not feeling too good.

(**THOMAS** *begins to get a little unsteady on his feet.* **ARTHUR** *comes to his aid.*)

ARTHUR. Let's go, Thomas.

THOMAS. I think I mixed my malts.

ARTHUR. Let's get you home.

(**ARTHUR** *helps* **THOMAS** *out of the house. For a moment,* **JULIA** *is alone in the room until…*)

(**THERESA** *enters from the kitchen with a paper cup of water and a towel over her shoulder. She has heard everything.*)

JULIA. Mom, let me –

(**THERESA** *approaches* **JULIA** *and throws the glass of water in her face.*)

Mom, please!

(**THERESA** *begins hitting* **JULIA** *with the paper cup and towel.*)

THERESA. *(pushing her)* Get out of my house!

JULIA. Mom, please!

THERESA. Now!

(*Finally,* **JULIA** *allows* **THERESA** *to push her out of the house.*)

Out! Out! Get out of my house!

(**THERESA** *slams the door shut as the weight of what has just transpired seems to almost crush her.*)

(*Lights out.*)

Scene Five

(Lights up on **THOMAS** *and* **GEORGE** *hanging out in another part of the park. It is the next day.* **GEORGE** *is flexing for* **THOMAS**. **THOMAS** *is wearing his work uniform for the Burger Barn. He looks very hung over and has a detached look about him.* **GEORGE** *does not look bigger at all.)*

GEORGE. So what you think?

THOMAS. I think you look exactly the same as you did before you started taking them.

GEORGE. I do not.

THOMAS. You do. I think you've bought a case of placebos, a case of nothing.

GEORGE. I'm getting bigger.

THOMAS. Dumber.

GEORGE. Jealous.

THOMAS. If you say so.

GEORGE. You don't have to be such a jerk about it.

THOMAS. How would you like me to be about it, George?

GEORGE. Never mind.

(Pause. Things settle until…)

How are things with your Dad?

THOMAS. It's good. He gives me my space and he wasn't lying about my room. It's exactly how I left it.

GEORGE. Holy time capsule, Batman.

THOMAS. Exactly.

GEORGE. Your Mom just let you leave?

THOMAS. Yeah, this whole Carla thing. She thought I needed some space. She thought being around him might be good for me. A male influence.

GEORGE. Is that what they refer to your Dad as? Male influence? That doesn't even make sense.

THOMAS. *(shrugging)* Yeah, I guess it doesn't. Fuck it, though, you know? Get out of the house for awhile. Clear my head and stuff.

GEORGE. Huh. You still can't talk about things with Carla?

THOMAS. Nope.

GEORGE. But you'll have to pay for it when you're eighteen?

THOMAS. Yup.

GEORGE. Why are you even bothering to work for her now?

THOMAS. She's still going to have my kid.

GEORGE. Yeah, but this whole thing is nonsense.

THOMAS. That's what I keep saying but no one wants to listen.

GEORGE. I listen.

THOMAS. I'm touched.

GEORGE. Dick.

THOMAS. You know what I mean.

GEORGE. Not really.

THOMAS. You can't help me, George. I mean, fine, sure, moral support, whatever. But the help I need has to come from Carla and she doesn't want anything to do with me.

GEORGE. Why did she even bother telling you?

THOMAS. I don't know. Maybe she likes to be near me.

GEORGE. I doubt that. You smell like dead cows these days.

(A beat and then the two begin playfully punching each other.)

THOMAS. Scum sucker.

GEORGE. Ass sniffer.

THOMAS. Jimmy hugger.

GEORGE. Pony pumper.

THOMAS. Goat gobbler.

GEORGE. Dildo smuggler.

THOMAS. Toe jam licker.

GEORGE. MILF jumping bastard.

*(***THOMAS***, in a explosion of movement, violently tackles ***GEORGE***, sending him to the ground. ***THOMAS*** has ***GEORGE*** pinned.)*

GEORGE. *(cont.)* Ow! Get off! Get the fuck off me, man.

(Finally, **THOMAS** *releases him.* **THOMAS** *gets up and sits back down.)*

GEORGE. *(cont.) (from the ground)* What the fuck was that about?

(Even **THOMAS** *doesn't know. Thinking quickly,* **THOMAS** *gets an idea.)*

THOMAS. I'm telling you. Those 'roids you bought aren't working. I wouldn't be able to do that if you were all juiced up.

*(***GEORGE** *thinks about this for a moment.)*

GEORGE. Oh yeah, you're right. Damn. They must have sold me a placebo.

*(***GEORGE** *gets up brushing himself off.)*

THOMAS. A whole case of placebos.

GEORGE. Oh well. You wanna get stoned?

THOMAS. No, I gotta work.

GEORGE. Really? You can't be a few minutes late?

THOMAS. Yeah, no, I gotta throw.

GEORGE. It's a free country. Remember?

THOMAS. I remember, George.

GEORGE. Free country's only as free as your choices. You don't "gotta" do anything. You can choose to stay and get high with me. You're free to choose. You just have to choose. Otherwise you're not exactly free, are you?

THOMAS. You a philosopher now?

GEORGE. Let's light up and find out. Choice is yours. Time to choose, my friend.

THOMAS. See you.

*(***THOMAS** *begins walking away.)*

GEORGE. Thomas.

THOMAS. Yeah?

GEORGE. Sure you don't want get high? You don't seem yourself today.

THOMAS. Maybe I'm diseased.

GEORGE. This usually treats it.

THOMAS. No. It'll pass.

GEORGE. You think so?

THOMAS. I do. Things pass.

(**THOMAS** *leaves the park.*)

GEORGE. *(shrugging)* Just means there's more for me, kid.

(**GEORGE** *takes out a joint and lights it. He begins to smoke it. After a beat he rubs his lower back, smarting a little.*)

That hurt.

(*Lights out.*)

Scene Six

(Lights up on the living room. Later that day. A knock on the door. THERESA enters from her bedroom and answers it. It's JULIA. THERESA leaves the door open and walks to a chair, sitting down. After a moment, JULIA walks into the house and closes the door behind her.)

(JULIA sits down in a chair. She takes a breath but nothing comes. Until finally...)

JULIA. This is difficult.

THERESA. Agreed.

JULIA. I've done things a certain way for a long time now. I've compartmentalized this. Put it in pieces. It's hard to look at it in one piece.

THERESA. Try.

JULIA. I only wanted to protect you.

THERESA. I'm the one who's supposed to protect you! Me! Not the other way around!

JULIA. I know.

THERESA. I'm your mother, Julia! When you needed me the most, why would you take that away from me?

JULIA. I was afraid.

THERESA. What do you think this does to me now?

JULIA. Mother, please.

THERESA. Every happy memory I had with that man, every good time I looked back on for comfort, now that he's gone, I have to now question and wonder and challenge – leaving me with questions that have no answers. Empty.

JULIA. It wasn't my fault.

THERESA. Why couldn't you tell me? Why?

JULIA. I don't know why. I just couldn't. I tried. It happened. It was happening.

THERESA. You could have told me. If I had known –

JULIA. What? What would you have done if you'd known?

THERESA. I would have been your protector!

JULIA. I wanted to tell you.

THERESA. But you didn't!

JULIA. No, I didn't! And then I was pregnant and I knew I could never tell you. Arthur was there, we had just started dating. I didn't love him, I barely knew him but it fit. It came together so easy. I could put it together – not how it really was – but this way. I could do that. I could take those pieces and put it together like that and just go away for a while – not forever – just a while. To clear my head.

THERESA. I loved your father.

JULIA. I know.

THERESA. I've been mourning him.

JULIA. I know!

THERESA. What am I supposed to do with all of this now? You hand all this to me now! You take away...how am I supposed to live next to that?

(**JULIA** *does not answer.* **THERESA** *looks on, wanting to ask something but feeling the dread that comes with it.*)

Was it once, Julia? Was it just the one time?

JULIA. *(shaking her head)* No.

THERESA. How many times?

JULIA. Please, don't.

THERESA. How many more, dammit? How many?

JULIA. More than once.

THERESA. What are we going to do?

JULIA. I don't know.

THERESA. What are we going to do?

JULIA. I don't know.

(*Lights out.*)

Scene Seven

(**CARLA** *is waiting for her bus at the bus stop. It is the next day, early evening.* **THOMAS** *enters wearing his Burger Barn uniform.*)

CARLA. Thomas, no.

THOMAS. It's okay.

CARLA. Do I have to change my bus route?

THOMAS. You're a lawyer. Why are you even taking the bus?

CARLA. I'm being green.

THOMAS. What?

CARLA. Never mind. Just go away.

THOMAS. It's not like you can get pregnant while you're pregnant.

CARLA. That's not the – stop!

THOMAS. I just want to see you.

CARLA. I don't want to see you. Not anymore.

(**THOMAS** *stops.*)

THOMAS. You know you want me.

CARLA. We will never be together in that way again.

THOMAS. That's what you said the last time.

CARLA. I mean it this time.

(**THOMAS** *takes a step closer and* **CARLA** *takes red pepper spray out of her purse.*)

THOMAS. You're going to mace me?

CARLA. It's not mace, it's red pepper spray.

THOMAS. What's the difference?

CARLA. I can legally put you down with red pepper spray if you get any closer. I'll do it, Thomas.

THOMAS. I'm just looking for a little comfort.

CARLA. You're going to have to get that from someone else. Stay away from me.

THOMAS. Don't you want me? Am I so damaged that being with me is such a dead proposition? Is it that obvious?

CARLA. I have a rape whistle, too.

(**CARLA** *pulls out her rape whistle.*)

THOMAS. Did you go shopping today?

CARLA. I'll use them both, Thomas.

THOMAS. I'll just stand here until your bus comes.

CARLA. I wish you wouldn't, Thomas. I wish you would just go away.

THOMAS. I'm going to stand here.

CARLA. Don't follow me home again. I swear, I'll use this.

THOMAS. I'll just stand here. When the bus comes, I'll watch you get on it. Then I'll go to work.

CARLA. It's over between us.

THOMAS. I heard you the first two times.

CARLA. You can stand there as long as you want. It won't change anything.

THOMAS. Maybe I don't want to change anything. Maybe I just want to stand here.

CARLA. Then stand.

THOMAS. I will.

CARLA. I don't love you.

THOMAS. I'm only fifteen. I don't know what love is anyway.

(*The two stand there, looking at each other, at an impasse.*)

(*Lights out.*)

Scene Eight

(It is later that evening. **THOMAS** *sits outside of Burger Barn in the parking lot, still wearing his uniform. He takes out a joint and begins smoking. After a few moments,* **THERESA** *comes out. She watches* **THOMAS** *smoke until...)*

THERESA. I have to admit Thomas, I am very disappointed by this.

THOMAS. Theresa.

THERESA. Very disappointed.

*(***THOMAS***, startled, puts out the joint and throws it on the ground. Finally...)*

THOMAS. I don't do it a lot.

THERESA. What's that?

THOMAS. I don't get high all that much. Just every once in a while. I know people say it's a "gateway drug" but I'm very content to just let it be what it –

*(***THERESA*** *waves for* **THOMAS** *to be quiet as she walks over to sit down next to him.)*

THERESA. Oh for heaven's sake, Thomas. I'm not talking about the pot.

THOMAS. You're not?

THERESA. No, I'm talking about the fact that you're sitting around the parking lot of Burger Barn like some kind of "home body."

THOMAS. I think you might mean, "home boy." Not "body."

THERESA. Very disappointing.

THOMAS. I thought you were upset about the...

THERESA. The pot?

THOMAS. Yeah.

THERESA. They're your brains, Thomas. You want to muck them up, the world can always use another day laborer.

(beat)

THERESA. *(cont.)* How are things at Arthur's house?

THOMAS. Fine. He's a lot looser than you guys.

THERESA. I'm sure he is.

(**THOMAS** *doesn't respond.*)

Are you all right over there?

THOMAS. I'm fine. He's starting to drink a lot again. I may have reminded him how much alcohol he has in that bar of his.

THERESA. Your mother was only trying to protect you. I think she was trying to protect us both.

THOMAS. Why would anyone ever need to be protected from the truth?

(**THERESA** *doesn't answer.*)

THERESA. You on a break?

THOMAS. No, I got off a little while ago.

THERESA. And you're still here?

THOMAS. Yeah. I'm just sitting. I sit here sometimes. I sit and think. It's mostly quiet. I can really feel the area, I can feel the whole parking lot, when it gets this quiet. Sometimes that helps me think...when I can feel the area I'm in. Things don't seem so...confusing.

THERESA. Ah, yes, those things...they do get confusing.

(**THOMAS** *looks up, finally noticing* **THERESA**'s *black eye.*)

THOMAS. What happened to your eye?

THERESA. I moved my head during one of my botox injections.

THOMAS. Ouch.

THERESA. Pretty much.

THOMAS. Maybe it's time to re-think some of that.

THERESA. Well, let's not get carried away. Nothing unacceptable about a little collateral damage. Besides, I know how old I am. I'm at peace with that. It's everyone else who should mind their own pie hole. *Hint.*

(Silence. Finally...)

THOMAS. I look like him. Don't I?

(**THERESA** *looks at* **THOMAS** *and she sees the resemblance, perhaps for the first time. This is not easy.*)

THERESA. You do. I can see him in you.

THOMAS. Does that make it hard for you to look at me?

THERESA. No...no, Thomas, that's not what makes any of this so hard.

THOMAS. It makes it hard for Arthur. I can tell.

(**THERESA** *doesn't respond. Finally...*)

THERESA. When he was alive – this was years ago – we had a mouse problem. We were pretty sure it was just the one mouse unless they had it worked out in shifts – I'm not sure how mice plan these things. Samuel, my husband Samuel, decided to buy a glue trap and set it where we normally saw the little brown thing creep about. I had heard glue traps were cruel so I was a little tentative about it but Samuel insisted it was just a rodent and it had to be done. Anyway, one night, I awoke to hear this...squeaking sound. I looked for Samuel but he wasn't in bed, so I put on my robe and followed the squeaking sounds and I found Samuel in his pajamas hunched over the glue trap that he had cut open and, with a spoon, very tenderly separating this wide eyed, brown, little mouse from the trap. And the mouse squeaked and squeaked but Samuel pressed on, little by little, delicately but firmly freeing this little, helpless mouse. I sat there and watched him – it seemed like hours. When he finally got the mouse free, patches of its' fur were stripped away. You could see parts of its' skin exposed and raw. He opened the front door and the mouse very slowly, very gingerly limped its' way out of our house. I watched Samuel stand there for a while, looking out the open door, watching the mouse hobble away. I snuck back to the bedroom and he never mentioned the moment to me. We didn't have a mouse problem after that – our little friend was either the only one or word traveled fast. But I never forgot that. I never forgot how tender and sensitive, how deeply caring he was. That's how I remember him now: a warm, sensitive, deeply caring man who was raping our daughter. That's what's hard for me, Thomas.

THOMAS. Am I like him?

THERESA. No.

THOMAS. You think I'm gonna be like him? Eventually? Whatever made him who he was, you think that's gonna follow me, find me?

THERESA. You will never be like him. I know you well enough to know that.

THOMAS. Who am I?

THERESA. You're loved, Thomas.

THOMAS. I'm only fifteen. What would I know about that?

THERESA. You know enough.

(THOMAS *looks away. Then…*)

THOMAS. How come you're here? How come my Mom isn't?

THERESA. Your mother isn't as strong as she'd like to be. I'm not sure anyone really is.

THOMAS. You're here.

THERESA. Yes.

(THOMAS *tries to absorb this…*)

THOMAS. I'm really confused.

THERESA. Welcome.

THOMAS. What am I supposed to do?

THERESA. You…begin.

THOMAS. What am I supposed to do after that?

(*Silence. Then…*)

You can't help me with this, can you?

THERESA. (*shaking her head*) I'm a little out of my depth, too.

(THOMAS *gets up to leave.*)

THOMAS. *(cold)* Okay, see you.

THERESA. Thomas.

> (**THOMAS** *stops and looks back.*)

I know it must be difficult to imagine yourself back with me and your mother. I know, in some ways, it must be easier, to be with your father. But we miss you and as tough as it may be for you – for us, too – there will always be a place for you.

> (**THOMAS** *exits.*)

> (*Lights out.*)

Scene Nine

(Lights up.)

(At the park. It is the following Sunday. **ARTHUR** *drinks from a bottle in a paper bag – he's sloppy drunk.* **THOMAS** *stares out. No food.)*

ARTHUR. ...and not for nothing, but you can't get all "the glass is half empty or full" about it because if the glass is filled with piss, who the fuck cares if it's half empty or half full. It's *piss!* You can't put a spin on urine, you know?

THOMAS. Women –

ARTHUR. Suck, Thomas! You get that now, you'll be okay. They really, really suck. They're manipulative, cold, and completely damaged! Okay, okay maybe it's not their fault. Fine I'll admit it. Let's not make them *evil.* It's not their fault. Someone else is to blame. Society. *Cosmo.* I do not blame them for being faulty. But they still are, Thomas. It's like you go to the store and you want to buy a wooden duck. Right?

THOMAS. A duck?

ARTHUR. Yeah, you need a duck. So you get in your car and you go to the store and it's a real long way away. But you get there. You arrive and you walk into the store and you go to the wooden duck aisle only to find out that some four year old with *down syndrome* has just picked up the last one and threw it down on the ground and so now instead of waddling in a straight line, it just sort of gimps around in a circle and makes a funny gurgling sound. And that's the problem! See? I'm screwed! And do you want to know why?

THOMAS. Why?

ARTHUR. Because I need the duck! Get it? I need the damn duck, okay? I am not ashamed to admit that. I saved the money. I've been a good guy. I came all the way to the store. I want the damn duck. I want to buy the wooden fucking duck!

But there is no way in hell I'm gonna buy a wooden

duck that can't walk in a straight line, Thomas! I don't care. I won't do it. I'm not buying some gimpy, gurgling duck that's gonna hobble in a circle. I don't care how much I need the goddamn thing! I don't care how lonely this leaves me! I'm done! I'm through! I'm going duckless!

(ARTHUR looks to THOMAS.)

ARTHUR. *(cont.)* Your Mom's a fucking duck.

THOMAS. She lied to me.

ARTHUR. Hey, welcome to the club. She lied to me, too. What are you going to do, T? Women are liars. But don't worry, I've been dealing with this particular lie for a few years now. I know how to manage it. How to keep it in its little place.

THOMAS. But didn't you say before how strength –

ARTHUR. You and I are going to be just fine. I know all the angles and cheats. Fuck dealing with this bullshit. You and I are going to start anew.

THOMAS. But you said –

ARTHUR. You and me. We'll circumvent this fuck rabbit and get on with some living. You and me. Living outside all this…noise. Fucking noise.

(THOMAS looks at his father, deciding something.)

THOMAS. Maybe this isn't such a good idea.

ARTHUR. What's that? What did you…

THOMAS. Maybe I should go stay with Theresa and Mom for a while. Give you a break.

ARTHUR. What did you say?

THOMAS. I'm just saying, I know, it's a lot of pressure for you seeing me and you're doing it when you're not technically my father.

ARTHUR. I will always be your…regardless of blood. I put my time in here. I sacrificed my goddamn everything for you. That makes me your father by default…there are rules…don't you try and take that…

THOMAS. I've been thinking about that.

ARTHUR. I won't allow it.

THOMAS. You don't have a say.

ARTHUR. I'll stop you. I'll physically stop you for your own good.

(**THOMAS** *stands up.*)

THOMAS. *(menacing)* I'll beat your ass.

ARTHUR. What did you say to me?

THOMAS. I said, I'll beat your ass, old man. I'll beat you until my hands hurt and when I'm through pounding on you, I'll go have dinner like it was nothing.

(**ARTHUR** *can't believe what* **THOMAS** *has said. He is both shocked and a little afraid.*)

ARTHUR. How can you talk to me like…I'm your…I'm like your father…

THOMAS. I've been thinking about that, Arthur.

ARTHUR. Don't call me – it's true. I'm your –

THOMAS. I know why Mom stopped being "special" to you now. But she couldn't have truly been "special" in the first place because you're not married anymore.

ARTHUR. Thomas, it's not as simple as –

THOMAS. There are three different kinds of women. You said that.

ARTHUR. Yeah, but –

THOMAS. If she wasn't a "special one" and I know she wasn't a "fuck buddy" then she was an "ecto-plasm girl." Doesn't that make her an "ecto-plasm girl" by default? The way you talk about her. In the end, even if you didn't know it at the time, isn't that what she ultimately became? If she wasn't "special." If she was your "ecto-plasm girl" then I'm not your son on any level.

ARTHUR. You are my son! Maybe not bio…don't fucking… you're my son!

THOMAS. No, I'm not your son. I'm your stain, Arthur. All these years, that's who I've been to you. To Mom. And I don't know where that leaves me, but I can tell that it shouldn't leave me here. For your sake as much as mine.

ARTHUR. You don't know what you're…

THOMAS. This seems like the right thing.

ARTHUR. You don't know how to deal with this…thing that
you have now.

THOMAS. I'll learn.

ARTHUR. You need me.

THOMAS. No, I don't.

ARTHUR. Don't take this from me, Thomas.

THOMAS. It's already been taken.

ARTHUR. You traitor.

THOMAS. I'll call when things calm down. Until then, no
more Sundays.

ARTHUR. Little shit.

THOMAS. In fact, let's cancel Sundays. If I ever want to
see you again, I'll let you know. You don't need to be
around me anyway. I'll just leave a mark.

ARTHUR. Ungrateful…

THOMAS. Gangs are always rolling drunks out here so you
should leave now while it's still light outside.

ARTHUR. Fuck you!

THOMAS. Goodbye, Arthur.

(**THOMAS** *exits the park.*)

(**ARTHUR**'s *alone.*)

ARTHUR. You little bastard! I got your fucking number!
I know where you're going! I see it all! Ungrateful.
Unworthy. Just like your fucking…

(**ARTHUR** *pushes himself to his feet.*)

It'll never come off of you, T! Never gonna come
off! You're tattooed! Everyone's gonna know! Everyone's gonna see you and they're all going to stay away
because of it! I fucking see you! I see you, you little
fucking stain!

(**ARTHUR** *has spent himself.*)

I see you.

(*Lights out.*)

Scene Ten

(Lights up on the living room. It is later that same day.)

*(**JULIA** is setting the table. She goes to set up **THOMAS**' place and stops, realizing what she's done. She stands there for a moment, looking a little lost. **THERESA** notices this and puts a hand on her shoulder. They have a moment, **JULIA** mostly in resistance about it, before resuming their place setting.)*

(There's a knock on the door.)

*(**THERESA** goes to the door and opens it. It's **CARLA**.)*

THERESA. Carla. We weren't expecting you.

CARLA. No.

JULIA. Carla.

CARLA. May I come in?

THERESA. Of course.

*(**CARLA** enters.)*

CARLA. Is Thomas here?

THERESA. No he's –

JULIA. Thomas is spending time with his father for awhile.

*(**CARLA** enters. **THERESA** closes the door behind her. There's an awkwardness, until...)*

THERESA. Would you like to sit down?

CARLA. Thank you.

*(**CARLA** sits down at the dining table.)*

JULIA. We're going to have dinner soon.

CARLA. I won't be long.

JULIA. That's not what I meant.

CARLA. Oh, no, okay.

JULIA. I mean, if you'd like to...

CARLA. No, no. Thank you, though.

THERESA. Is everything all right?

CARLA. I wanted to stop by and let you know that I was going to be leaving for awhile.

JULIA. Leaving?

CARLA. The law firm I work for has several offices across the country and they just had an opening out West. I've got some family out there, too, so –

JULIA. You're just going to go?

CARLA. For awhile.

THERESA. Thomas doesn't know?

CARLA. No, actually, I haven't seen him since…it's been a while.

JULIA. He may have a hard time with that, you know?

CARLA. I'm going to have a hard time with it. Uprooting, leaving what I know. It's not like –

JULIA. We may have a hard time with it as well.

CARLA. Why would you…?

JULIA. Look, just because this wasn't…

(**JULIA** *stops herself. Tension.*)

THERESA. I think what Julia means –

CARLA. I'm just trying to do what's best.

JULIA. And we're not?

CARLA. No, that's not what I mean.

THERESA. What do you mean?

CARLA. For me. I need to go away because it's best for me.

JULIA. There will come a time when –

CARLA. Can we address it, then?

JULIA. What's wrong with now?

THERESA. Julia.

JULIA. No, I'd like to know. You want Thomas to take care of this baby and yet you won't even be here when the time comes?

CARLA. Why do you even care?

JULIA. *(raising her voice)* It involves Thomas. I care.

CARLA. *(raising her voice)* Don't you raise your voice to me.

JULIA. Don't think you know what's best for Thomas.

(**CARLA** *stands up from the table.* **JULIA** *follows suit, the fight escalating.*)

THERESA. *(rising from her chair)* Settle down everyone.

CARLA. It was a mistake coming here.

*(**CARLA** moves towards the door as **JULIA** moves to her.)*

JULIA. Where do you think you're going?

CARLA. I'm leaving. I know what's best for me. I'm not –

JULIA. He's already living with his father, do you want him to start following you across the country, too?

THERESA. Julia.

CARLA. Thomas is not my main concern.

JULIA. Maybe he is.

THERESA. Julia, stop!

CARLA. What does that mean?

JULIA. Maybe you're just trying to lure him out west away from us.

CARLA. Have you lost your mind?

THERESA. Julia! Let it go!

(A moment. They all stand there. An uneasy pause. Until…)

CARLA. I really should go.

*(**CARLA** moves to exit.)*

THERESA. Carla.

CARLA. Yes?

*(**THERESA** doesn't know quite what to say until…)*

THERESA. *(reaching)* Have you…thought about whether you want a boy or a girl?

CARLA. What? Oh. I don't…I don't know.

THERESA. Rather it be a surprise?

CARLA. So much of this has been a surprise already it only makes sense.

THERESA. Well, for your sake, let's hope it's a girl.

CARLA. I'll take healthy.

THERESA. Healthy's enough.

(beat)

CARLA. I do want us all to feel good about this.

JULIA. You think that's possible?

CARLA. I don't know. I'd like it to be.

(This last statement hangs there until...)

THERESA. I'd like a drink.

*(**THERESA** moves towards the kitchen.)*

JULIA. Interesting segue, Mom.

THERESA. Carla?

CARLA. Okay, sure. Juice for me.

THERESA. Mimosa has juice in it, I think.

CARLA. Don't tempt me. I just might.

THERESA. Fair enough.

*(**THERESA** exits towards the kitchen. **CARLA** moves to **JULIA**.)*

CARLA. Julia...

(It hangs there for a moment until...)

JULIA. I know.

*(**THERESA** re-enters with two bottles of champagne.)*

THERESA. Shall we go Moet or Taittinger?

CARLA. Seriously, make mine a virgin.

(Everyone freezes at the unintentional double meaning until...they laugh, albeit a bit uncomfortably.)

*(**THOMAS** enters from the front door, carrying his bag.)*

JULIA. Thomas, we weren't expecting you.

CARLA. Hello, Thomas.

*(**THOMAS** shuts the door, his back to his everyone.)*

THERESA. Are you all right?

*(**THOMAS** turns around, revealing that he is sobbing quietly but uncontrollably.)*

*(They watch **THOMAS** as he sobs. After a moment, the sobbing concludes.)*

(**THOMAS** *takes a deep stabilizing breath and looks to* **THERESA**. *He then walks towards* **JULIA** *stopping just in front of her. He looks directly at her, confronting her with an intense stare.* **JULIA** *returns his stare.*)

THOMAS. Okay. Okay.

(*The two continue their stare as* **THOMAS** *releases his bag. It hits the floor with a resounding thud. No one blinks.*)

(*Lights out.*)

End of Play

PROP/SET/SOUND LIST

ACT ONE
Scene One

Sound: Gunshots.
Props: 2 Hot Dogs. 2 Bottled Waters.
Set: Park Bench.

Scene Two

Props: 3 Dinner Plates and Place Settings. Water. Salad. Vegetables.
Roast. (food items optional)

Set: (Dining/Living Room. Dining Room table with four chairs. Two
Sofa Chairs. Picture Wall: Pictures of Julia, Theresa, Thomas and
Theresa's deceased husband, Samuel)

Scene Three

Props: 2 Book Bags. Rolling Papers. Fake Marijuana. Matches. Stick.
Set: Makeshift Bench. (2 beat up plastic buckets, piece of lumber)
Sound: Gunshot.

Scene Four

Set: Dining Room Table.
Props: Tea Set for Two, i.e., tea, cups and saucers, milks and sugar

Scene Five

Props: Coffee Cup.
Set: Park Bench

Scene Six

Props: Tea Set for Three (i.e., tea, cups and saucers, milks and sugar)
Crossword Puzzle and Pen. Notebook, School Textbook and Pencil.
Briefcase.

Set: Dining/Living Room.

Scene Seven

Set: Park Bench.

ACT TWO
Scene One

Props: Purse. Glass of Water. Cup of Tea. Duffle Bag.
Set: Dining/Living Room.

Scene Two

Sound: Gunshot.

Set: Park Bench

Scene Three

Set: Bus Stop Sign.

Props: Briefcase.

Scene Four

Set: Dining/Living Room

Props: Laundry and Laundry Basket. Cup of Tea. Glass of Water. Plastic Cup of Water. Towel.

Scene Five

Props: 2 Book Bags.

Set: Makeshift Bench. 2 beat up plastic buckets, piece of lumber

Scene Six

Props: Red Pepper Spray. Rape Whistle. Briefcase.

Set: Bus Stop Sign.

Scene Seven

Set: Dining/Living Room

Scene Eight

Set: Burger Barn Sign. Milk Crates.

Props: Fake Marijuana Cigarette. Lighter. Bag of Garbage.

Scene Nine

Set: Park Bench.

Props: Whiskey Bottle in Brown Bag. Duffle Bag.

Scene Ten

Set: Dining/Living Room

Props: 2 Dinner plates and place settings. Duffle Bag. Briefcase.

Set Design by Eddy Trotter

Set Design by Eddy Trotter

Also by
Tony Glazer...

Safe

Please visit our website **samuelfrench.com** for complete
descriptions and licensing information